GUITAR *signature licks*

2ND

CARLOS SANTANA

BY WOLF MARSHALL

Cover photo by Jeffrey Mayer

"Smooth" analysis by Chad Johnson

PLAYBACK+
Speed • Pitch • Balance • Loop

To access audio visit:
www.halleonard.com/mylibrary

Enter Code
3058-4167-7443-0983

ISBN 978-1-4950-8224-5

7777 W. BLUEMOUND RD. P.O. BOX 13819 MILWAUKEE, WI 53213

Visit Hal Leonard Online at
www.halleonard.com

CONTENTS

INTRODUCTION

Carlos Santana is one of those rare musicians who truly speak through their instrument. His language is sound—singing notes, emotional phrasing, and stirring melodies forming words, sentences, and paragraphs; his vocabulary is a rainbow of styles merging blues, rock, jazz, and Latin idioms; and his message is one of communication, spirituality, and healing. As a guitarist, he is a unique artist. In his hands, ideas become musical statements—events virtually devoid of cliche and gimmickry woven into the tapestry of a song's whole. It is interesting to note that both the Santana guitar sound and band sound have remained distinctive and indeed exemplary even though the equipment and personnel have changed many times over the years.

Carlos Santana began his musical journey in Autlan Jalisco Mexico de Navarro, Mexico. Encouraged by his father (a mariachi violinist), he started on the violin at the age of five. Though he allegedly disliked the instrument—more accurately, disliked his ability on the violin—he learned to play several classical compositions by Beethoven, and Von Suppe's "Poet and Peasant Overture." Perhaps like fellow fretboard innovator Allan Holdsworth, Santana was subliminally affected by the sustain and legato qualities of the violin, as these very attributes have been manifested on the guitar in his own individual style. Carlos later decided on the guitar, and learned the basics of chording and some Mexican folk songs from his father. In 1955, the Santana family moved to Tijuana, and Carlos found himself gravitating toward the blues and rock sounds emanating from the nightclubs in the local red light district. The music of B.B. King, Ray Charles, Bobby Blue Bland, and Little Richard caught his ear and, subsequently through his contact with guitarist Javier Batiz, he learned to play blues guitar at around eleven years of age. A short time later, Carlos turned pro and was playing American Top 40 and R&B for pay in T.J.'s notorious strip clubs and bars.

Santana's move to San Francisco in 1961 coincided with the musical renaissance beginning in Haight-Ashbury. He was drawn to the growing blues movement, and was profoundly influenced by both the traditional sounds of Muddy Waters, Jimmy Reed, and Otis Rush; and the more modern approach of the Paul Butterfield Blues Band (featuring Mike Bloomfield and Elvin Bishop on guitars), and, later, Eric Clapton on *Fresh Cream*. In late 1966, he formed the first of many Santana Blues Bands after hooking up with keyboardist Gregg Rolie (later of Journey fame). The Santana Blues Band made its official debut at the legendary Fillmore West in 1968, though Carlos had been attracting attention for a year or so prior to that performance.

1969 was the year of Santana. While leading his own electric blues groups and gigging around the Bay Area, he guested on *The Live Adventures of Mike Bloomfield and Al Kooper*, though previously unknown. Santana dropped the Blues Band tag, added Latin percussion—Mike Carrabello (congas) and Jose Chepito Areas (timbales) to the nucleus of Rolie (organ/piano/vocals), Dave Brown (bass), Michael Shrieve (drums), and himself on guitar—and in the process, created a new direction and sound in rock music. Santana appeared on the highly visible "Ed Sullivan Show"—the program credited with introducing the Beatles and the Stones to American audiences. Their debut album, *Santana*, released in 1969, went platinum within a year and remained on the Billboard charts for over two years. The exciting live rendition of "Soul Sacrifice," performed at Woodstock in August and seen on the Woodstock documentary, propelled the band to international notoriety.

This book primarily focuses on the definitive tracks of the early Santana band period, roughly from 1969–1972, in which they made their initial but indelible mark on the face of music history.

THE SANTANA SOUND

Though a staunch Paul Reed Smith advocate since the nineties, Carlos Santana derived his signature sound from a variety of guitars in the early days of the Santana band. In the late sixties, when he first formed the Santana Blues Band, he favored a '63 Gibson SG Special.

Santana employed a number of Les Pauls and SGs throughout the early seventies, including a cherry sunburst Les Paul Standard and a white three-pickup SG Custom. He played a Gibson L-6S (with a 6-position rotary switch for extra tonal variations) briefly in the mid 1970s before switching to Yamaha solid bodies (SG-2000 models) for the remainder of the decade.

Santana discovered Paul Reed Smith electrics in the early eighties and these remain his primary electric guitars. He prefers his custom-made guitars by Paul Reed, with custom humbucking pickups. He has been known, on occasion, to use a Fender Stratocaster ("She's Not There") or a Gibson Byrdland arch-top "jazz guitar" (as on the *Amigos* album), and expresses a fondness for his Yamaha nylon-string acoustic during those rare unplugged moments.

Carlos has played with large, triangular, heavy-gauge nylon picks since his club days in Tijuana. He strung his guitars with Ernie Ball Super Slinkies (a .008 set) in the late sixties but switched to a mixed set (Gibson treble: .009, .011 and .015 plus Ernie Ball bass: .024, .036 and .042) by the early seventies. Today Carlos uses the same style picks, custom-made for him by Dunlop, endorses and uses D' Addario strings (gauge .009–.042).

On the early Santana records, Carlos played through beefed-up Fender Twin Reverb amps. He never utilized a fuzz box, gain boost, or sustain device of any sort to attain his legendary harmonic feedback sound, preferring instead to do it "the old-fashioned way"—by sheer volume, and proximity and angle to the amplifier.

In the mid seventies, his brother, Jorge Santana (a fine guitarist in his own right) turned him on to a Mesa Boogie amp. Carlos has been a devout user of the Boogies ever since. His lead tone comes from an early Mark I combo model—probably one of the very first production units, loaded with Ruby 6L6 power tubes. For rhythm, he alternates between Marshalls (distorted rhythm) and Fender Twins (clean rhythm). His effect setup is spare—the only gadgets Carlos uses with any regularity are a wah-wah pedal and an occasional chorus box or octave divider.

DISCOGRAPHY

The first two Santana records, *Santana* and *Abraxas* (CK 30130), are bonafide classics and are indispensable in any contemporary record collection. The sound quality is exceptional on the SBM Master Sound collector's edition of *Santana* (CK 64212), and makes that reissue especially worth looking for.

The beautifully packaged and informative 1995 anthology, *Dance of the Rainbow Serpent* (C3K 64605), is a highly recommended three-disc collection featuring the definitive early material, later releases, live performances including the 1969 Woodstock version of "Soul Sacrifice," previously unavailable tracks with Larry Graham, Vernon Reid, and Chester Thompson as well as collaborations with John McLaughlin, John Lee Hooker, and Weather Report. The compilation, *Santana's Greatest Hits* (CK 33050), originally released in 1974 is also a serviceable introduction to the classic Santana band cuts.

Also a must is the *Carlos Santana—Influences* video (DCI VH0211), in which Santana chronicles the effect three of his idols had on him and on his music. Included is rare live performance footage of Wes Montgomery, Bola Sete, and Gabor Szabo—worth the price of admission alone.

The titles in this book came from the following records:

SANTANA (1969)
Evil Ways, Jingo, Soul Sacrifice, Persuasion

ABRAXAS (1970)
Black Magic Woman, Gypsy Queen, Oye Como Va, Incident At Neshabur, Se A Cabo, Samba Pa Ti, Hope You're Feeling Better

SANTANA III (1971)
Toussaint L'Overture

CARAVANSERAI (1972)
Song of the Wind

SUPERNATURAL (1999)
Smooth

THE RECORDING

Editor's Note: Follow the audio icons ◆ in the book. The track icons are placed after the figure numbers at the top of each figure. When more than one icon appears after a figure, the first track listed is a recording of the figure in full. All other track numbers listed are notable individual guitar parts played slower.

Wolf Marshall: guitar

John Nau: organ, piano

Michael Della Gala: bass guitar

Mike Sandberg: drums, percussion

Glenn Nishida: audio engineer (rhythm tracks)

Wolf Marshall: audio engineer (guitars and mixdown)

Produced by Wolf Marshall

INTERVIEW BY JOHN STIX

Carlos Santana's guitar work is among the most graceful and honest in rock. That this remains as true today as it did over 40 years ago, when his band burst onto the national scene as a highlight of the original Woodstock festival, comes as no surprise to fans of the electric guitar. From soaring melodies to throat ripping riffs, Carlos Santana's guitar work stands out in the crowd. Any crowd. Melodic grace, crying sustain and treacherous blues/rock solos have made him one of the electric guitar's most acclaimed and lyrical stylists.

Santana is also one of the few musicians who is just as eloquent speaking about his music as he is playing it. Carlos was a naturally insightful guide when asked to provide us with a tour of his greatest hits. Beyond anecdotal history, he revealed that some of his best-known moments of instrumental lyricisim actually had their roots in poems and lyrics. Having known Carlos for close to 20 years, this was news to me, but not a surpise from the man who claims Dionne Warwick and Aretha Franklin as influences on his six-string singing. Now using the "1812 Overture" to inspire "Soul Sacrifice" is another story—and one worth learning.

WHEN WAS THE FIRST TIME YOU HEARD "BLACK MAGIC WOMAN?"

It was in Fresno, California, at a soundcheck. Gregg Rolie brought the cassette in and said, "You'll really like this song." He wanted to know if we could try it. I remember I liked the way he (Peter Green in Fleetwood Mac) did it, but I didn't like it for us. He starts with a different kind of chord in the blues. Now when I listen to it I like it. But back then I said, "Let's do something different to it." So we started messing around with it and basically put more of a Calypso, African/Cuban thing on it.

BUT THE INSTRUMENTAL MELODY IN THE BEGINNING IS THE SAME.

The descending Wes Montgomery kind of melody is just basically "All Your Love" by Otis Rush. If you take the line "got a black magic woman" and put in the words "all your lovin' is lovin'," you can hear that he changed the chords and made it so it's not ripping anybody off. It's like taking a seed and making a different tree with it, just like Luther Burbank used to do with roses.

He was a botanist who would crossbreed roses. The rose might be all white but just the tip would be red. Peter Green did something to it and we did something different to it. And people say, "Well it's got to be a Santana song." It's more Santana than Fleetwood Mac.

HOW DID "GYPSY QUEEN" GET GRAFTED ON THERE?

I'm pretty sure it was my idea to segue the two songs. At that time all I was playing was Gabor Szabo. I basically felt that I needed to escape from the B.B. King galaxy. Everybody, from Otis Rush to Buddy Guy to Mike Bloomfield to Peter Green, was playing B.B. King. So I needed to find my own thing away from B.B. I love him, but I felt like I needed to get out from under his spell. Gabor Szabo, Bola Sete, and Wes Montgomery got me out of it. I love the blues to this day. It's just that I didn't want to be an echo of somebody else. I wanted to find my own fingerprints. It's just like kids do today. You listen to this and that and by the time you sweat it, if you know how to do it, it comes out like you. Like Miles Davis. You can hear Billie Holliday and Louis Armstrong coming out of him.

DOES THE ORIGINAL "GYPSY QUEEN" BY GABOR SZABO SOUND AS SIMILAR AS "BLACK MAGIC WOMAN" DOES TO FLEETWOOD MAC?

No. Basically his is more acoustic with Ron Carter (bass). It's more subdued. Our "Gypsy Queen" has more of a Fleetwood Mac or Jimi Hendrix kind of energy.

IS THERE MORE TO THE ORIGINAL SONG THAN WHAT YOU PLAY?

Oh yeah, we played just little parts of it. In those days, they told us to edit everything. Originally we went to extremes. The first Santana band would play nothing but long jam songs. No bridge, no choruses, no intros, just long jams. Albert Gianquinto, who used to play piano with James Cotton, is the one who told us it would probably be better for our album if we just make songs three minutes long instead of eight or 12 minutes long. So that's why we edited.

DO YOU REMEMBER AT WHAT POINT YOU STARTED TO DEVELOP YOUR SUSTAIN?

Way before I cut the first album. As soon as I heard "Supernatural" by Peter Green. Then there was Jimi Hendrix with "Foxy Lady" and Jeff Beck's *Truth* album. I said, "Oh!" Plus it came easy for me because I used to play the violin. Instead of using a bow, I just mark the floor where there is an umbilical chord happening between the guitar and the amplifier.

DO YOU USE A VIOLIN VIBRATO, WHICH IS MORE HORIZONTAL THAN UP AND DOWN?

I think so. It's more sideways, like Allan Holdsworth or Santo and Johnny. Don't laugh, man, that stuff sounds really good today. I love Santo and Johnny.

I LOVE THE SOUND OF IT AND THE SINGING QUALITY.

Yeah, that's what it is. Peter Green is the one that really did it for me. You should know "Supernatural," because that song is the most regal song you could ever hear on sustain. In fact, for anybody who plays with sustain, if they listen to that song, it makes all of us regroup. It's like learning how to tackle somebody. When you hear sustain like that you can tackle somebody, bring them down. You can bring their guard down so they have to listen to the whole song. It's an incredible song; it's on the *Hard Road* album with John Mayall.

OF ALL THE DIFFERENT "BLACK MAGIC WOMAN/GYPSY QUEENS" THAT YOU'VE RECORDED, DO YOU HAVE A FAVORITE RENDITION?

I'm partial to all of them. Some people say the first one. It sounds fine, but I think the way we're doing it now gets it over, otherwise I wouldn't be doing it.

MY FAVORITE RECORDING IS THE LIVE ONE ON THE VIVA SANTANA! RECORD.

That was from a show in Montreal. That was a really good concert. Miles Davis said, "Sometimes there's one concert in 50 where you just show up and it all happens. You don't have to do anything." I think that was one of those concerts.

WHY DID YOU WANT A SECOND GUITAR PLAYER?

Because I heard a voice. It's the same question Miles Davis asked me. Miles never liked another guitar player in the band. So he was always on my case, "Why did you get that mother-fucker?" I just hear another sound. Plus, I don't have a big ego like a lot of people. I don't care whether it is Sonny Sharrock or Jeff Beck. If I hear a sound I go for it.

WHERE IS THE BEST NEAL SCHON? WAS IT ON A SANTANA RECORD?

Probably that "Everybody Is Everything" and "Song of the Wind," which we did as half and half. We both traded off a lot.

ON "SONG OF THE WIND" I STILL CAN'T HEAR WHERE ONE OF YOU LEAVES OFF AND THE OTHER TAKES OVER.

Well by that time he was coming more to my side. I wasn't going to go to his side, which is Eric Clapton. I love Eric Clapton and B.B. King, but I'm always looking to find my own fingerprints. You can trace me more to Gabor Szabo and singers. I used to sing "Never Gonna Give You Up" by George Butler, the original Ice Man. I used to listen to a lot of singers. Vernon Reid and I discussed how we listened a lot to Dionne Warwick. That's where we learned how to sing. She has a very beautiful middle path where she doesn't sound black or white. She just sounds like a soul. Like a glass of water with no color in it. I like that tone, I like that sound.

"SONG OF THE WIND" SOUNDS LIKE A COMPOSED SOLO. DID YOU WRITE IT OUT OR DID YOU REHEARSE IT AHEAD OF TIME?

No, Gregg Rolie and I started playing two chords, the same chords we used on "Incident at Neshabur" and everything else that I use, F to C (Fmaj7 to Cmaj7), and I just went a different kind of way. Then I started putting in all the things that I was listening to at that time, like "Love on a Two Way Street." When you listen to all those songs on *Caravanserai*, you can hear everything I used to listen to then from *Sketches of Spain* by Miles, to *First Light* by Freddie Hubbard. "Song of the Wind" is a melody and an improvisation. Basically, I would stick to a theme. That's the thread to dance around. Once you go out, then I'll find another thread. He'll find one and then I'll find one. It was kind of like running a relay with a baton. He passed it to me, and I was passing it to him.

FMAJ7 TO CMAJ7 RESONATE WITH YOU. WHAT DO THEY GIVE YOU?

To me it's like the Grand Canyon. You can never see the Grand Canyon the same way twice. It's always different. Within those two chords you could put "Fool on the Hill" by the Beatles and a million other songs and they all fit. It's the closest thing to that universal corridor when everything can be played.

NEAL MUST HAVE BEEN USING A LES PAUL ON "SONG OF THE WIND."

We both bought them at the same time. They looked like identical sunbursts. His got ripped off and I gave mine to Mr. Udo, who is the greatest promoter in Japan.

WHAT KIND OF AMP WERE YOU USING FOR CARAVANSIRAI?

Straight ahead two Fender Twins.

DID YOU HAVE AMP SETTINGS YOU STARTED WITH?

Just anything and everything to sustain without the pedals. I never like sustaining pedals.

WHAT WAS YOUR EQUIPMENT SETUP FOR ABRAXAS?

Pretty much Fender Twins and a Les Paul guitar.

WHAT WAS IT LIKE RECORDING SANTANA AND ABRAXAS?

Abraxas was all done very quickly at Wally Heiders Studio in San Francisco by Fred Catero. We were already doing the songs live. That was the good thing about the first band and album. Everything that we played we were already playing live, so by the time we went to the studio, we knew it. We were playing it almost like a year or something like that before we recorded most of those songs. That was basically the seeds of the first album. I remember we were in Boston, in Cambridge, walking around a week or two weeks before Woodstock, when it came out. Oh man! We liked the songs but we just hated the sound. Everything sounded kind of thin. It got messed up in the mastering.

THE WHOLE RECORD WAS DONE WITH A GIBSON AND THE FENDER TWIN AMPS.

The first one was pretty much done with the red Gibson SG you saw at Woodstock. The second one and third one and *Caravanserai* was with the Les Paul and always the Fender Twins. Not until the middle part of *Caravanserai* did I discover the Boogie amp. The Boogie came through with an extra knob for sustain, which was my idea. I said, "Can you add an extra knob so I can crank the first one to 10 and sustain, and bring the other one to 3 so it's not so loud?"

YOU WERE THE MASTER VOLUME MAN FOR BOOGIE?

To my recollection, I'm the one that suggested it to him, if he could do such a thing. To my surprise, he did it and he blew me away. It was just necessity. I don't know anything about ohms except chanting it! Other than that, I don't know nothing about wire. But I did know that it made sense to me that if you added a master volume that you could use one to control the actual volume and the other one to control the intensity of the sustain.

WHAT IS THE STORY BEHIND "EVIL WAYS?"

It's a Sonny Henry song by way of Willie Bobo. Bill Graham used to have a thing with Tito Puente and Willie Bobo and all those guys. He told Willie Bobo, "There's a band from San Francisco and I'm going to give them 'Evil Ways,' and they are going to take it further than you did." So he invited us to his office and he just played it for us. At first, it sounded a little foreign to us but once we played it, it was so natural. Like "Black Magic Woman." Some things just fit you so naturally. Thank you Bill Graham.

IT'S ALSO GM TO C, WHICH IS A VERY COMFORTABLE AREA FOR YOU.

It's pretty much like the Carole King thing, "It's Too Late," and all those songs which people were playing a lot in those days.

WAS "EVIL WAYS" RECORDED QUICKLY?

Yeah, that was recorded really quickly. That was the first album. The first album was done with everything within less then a week. I think in three days it was recorded and mixed. We didn't know that we could take our time and get better sounds with it. So everything was kind of rushed. We had opened enough times for Paul Butterfield and Creedence Clearwater Revival and everybody playing those songs that we really did know them. We didn't know about taking our time with the board and getting a better sound. I think we did the best with what we knew, what we had.

"I HOPE YOU'RE FEELING BETTER?"

It's a Gregg Rolie song. That's when I used a Marshall for the first time. That's a Gregg Rolie song, a Gregg Rolie approach. That's what he heard. You want me to go through a Marshall, cool. Crank it up, cool. "Mother's Daughter" is another Gregg Rolie song.

"INCIDENT AT NESHABUR" HAS ALWAYS BEEN AN IMPORTANT SONG FOR YOU.

I'm really fond of that song. It's got the same chord progression at the end of it as "Song of the Wind." The first part on the piano is kind of like Horace Silver. There were no lyrics but it was a pimp poem we chanted that ended the line with "Go ahead brother right on." It was a street slang thing.

YOU CHANTED IT IN THE STUDIO WHILE YOU WERE RECORDING THE OPENING CHORDS TO "INCIDENT?"

Yeah, that was an Albert Gianquinto thing. That was his intro and the second half was my part, where it slows down. We worked it out. I needed to go to that transition so when we slow it down, we put a kind of waltz-like descending line to get us into that progression of C into the F.

YOU AND JEFF BECK ARE SO MELODIC.

Jeff is a great player. He is somebody that can really give life to a tune. The other one is Eric Johnson. I'm waiting for him to play more songs. He is a very melodic cat. That's the whole thing, melodic and lyrical, like Miles.

"JINGO (JI·GO·LO·BA)" IS A STANDARD.

It's an Olatunji song in B minor.

HOW WERE YOU INTRODUCED TO IT?

By walking through Aquatic Park in San Francisco, where they have a bunch of conga players and people smoking pot and drinking wine and watching the ladies go by and playing blues. They always sang that song. Again, we put a guitar in there and the bass line. We did something different to it so it would sound different then Olatunji or the way the guys at the fountain in New York at Central Park or Aquatic Park do it. They still play that song if you go there. It's a very masculine song. Olatunji's album was called *Drums of Passion*. It's very sensual.

"OYE COMO VA?"

Is definitely something that I heard late at night. I knew without a shadow of a doubt that "Oye Como Va" was a party song. When you play it people are going to get up and dance. That's what it is, a party song like "Louie Louie."

TELL ME ABOUT "PERSUASION."

It's burning with funk. It was kind of like where Vernon Reid was going, more rock, almost like punk rock. The energy is very primitive.

"SAMBA PA TI" IS A SPECIAL SONG FOR YOU. YOU NAILED THAT ONE.

"Samba Pa Ti" is something that I wrote in New York City. We had just gotten back from our first trip to Europe and I had serious jet lag. When you are weak like that from jet lag, good things come in and bad things come in and out. You've got to be really careful. I was in a very fragile receptive mood. I heard this guy playing a saxophone outside of my window. He was trying to play bebop. After a while I looked out the window to see what it was and it was this guy who looked like he just got off a merry-go-round that was going 1,000 mph, so he couldn't stand up straight. You could tell the whole world was moving too fast on him. He was nodding back and forth. It broke my heart because he looked like me and he looked like everybody, every man that I know, in the sense that he didn't know what to put in his mouth: The bottle of booze from his pocket or the saxophone's mouthpiece to play. His mind couldn't decide. He would put the sax almost to his lips and then he put it out and he grabbed the bottle. He almost took a drink. He was moving around like he was dizzy. It just broke my heart. Because when I saw him I saw all of us battling on this planet. Because we are all doing time on this planet. So what I heard first was the poem. The poem went through every step in life you find, freedom from within. Freedom comes from within. So "Samba Pa Ti" is a way to get people out of that headlock from a demonic force. A demonic force is what makes a man be lost like that. So when I wrote the poem it went "through every step in life you find," it was a melody that was put to this poem. When I played it, I showed it to the guys and some of them said that's nice. When we went to record it, people didn't want to do it. To my recollection, that was the first time I actually pulled rank on the band and said this song goes in or I'm out, get somebody else kind of thing. I had to fight for it. Finally when everybody said, "Well you put it that way, I guess it's going to go." Once we did it, it was one take. Gregg and I. I'm really glad I did it because I hear a lot of people doing it like Ottmar Liebert. There's a story in there. You don't always have to have words in English or in Spanish. You can say a whole song just like "Europa" or "Samba Pa Ti" from beginning to end and it's a straight ahead melody thing, which now I hear Steve Vai is doing.

DO YOU HAVE A COMPLETE SET OF LYRICS TO "SAMBA PA TI?"

Basically it goes, "Through every step in life you find freedom from within, and if your mind should understand, woman love your man. Because everybody is searching for eternal peace. It is there, all you have to do is share." Those are the lyrics. I don't want anybody to sing it.

THERE IS ONE MOMENT IN THERE THAT IS CLASSIC. IT'S WHERE YOU SWITCH PICKUPS. IT'S A BONE CHILLER.

That's in the G to Am part. I did it because the treble pickup is like the alto or the soprano. The bass pickup is like a tenor. Once I couldn't hear anymore of that tenor tone, I just switched to the alto or the soprano, which is the more female. Treble is female, and, of course, bass is masculine. That's the way I always look at it. When I finished the solo the headphones were on my forehead and the back of my head instead of on my ears. I was bobbing and weaving and trying to complete the song without stopping, because it came in as one stream. I remember the first thing I asked everybody was "How was that?" I had no idea, man. It's like riding a black horse with no saddle. You just try to stay on it, which is really what it is, riding a solo. For an emotional solo, you've got to stay on it even if you think you'll fall off. I always look at it that way.

"TOUSSAINT L'OVERTURE" IS A JAMMING SONG.

Toussaint was the guy who defeated Napoleon before Waterloo. He was a black man who kicked Napoleon's butt. We wrote it for him. It is basically the same chorus…

AS "WALK DON'T RUN"…

And "California Dreaming," and "Hit the Road, Jack." It's the same chords. Those chords are, again, like a big old tunnel that a lot of songs can fit through.

IT WAS HARD FOR ME TO TELL IF IT WAS A PROGRESSION YOU JAMMED ON OR A MELODY SONG.

We always jam. But whatever we jam, there was always some kind of theme in it. That's the first thing that people told me when I started in Haight Ashbury. "Man, you are different. You are very melodic, very lyrical even though you are just jamming." They said, "We know that you don't know what you're doing, but its very lyrical." No matter how crazy things get, I always have to hear Aretha or Dionne Warwick singing in there. That's what keeps me melodic or thematic. Otherwise it just sounds like a bunch of notes and you lose me. You also lose the people.

WHAT WAS THE SEED FOR "SOUL SACRIFICE?"

It came from this conga player named Marcus Malone, and also from Aquatic Park where all the conga players hang out. Basically, he had a riff, and Gregg and I had another riff, and we were thinking more symphonic. We were listening to the "1812 Overture" a lot in those days. We would take acid and we used to play that to clean the house. You know hippies can get funky after a week. That was the only time I ever played classical music, when we hippies wanted to clean the house. Anything else wouldn't work because we just wouldn't clean the house. We'd just started tripping. We wouldn't start cleaning the house until we started listening to this classical music. Think the main melody to the "1812 Overture." Then, put in the rhythm guitar/organ part of "Soul Sacrifice;" yeah, that makes sense. It was the closest thing we ever got to European classical music.

IS THERE ANYTHING YOU WANT TO SAY ABOUT PERFORMING THESE SONGS LIVE?

You have to feel it. If you don't feel it, nobody is going to feel it. It don't matter whether you are playing "La Cucaracha," "A Love Supreme," or "Beethoven's 5th" or "9th," if you don't feel it, nobody is going to feel it. You have to be conscious of what you play. There is something that goes beyond the note and the chord. You have to be able to feel it. Otherwise other people are not going to feel it.

EVIL WAYS

(*Santana*, 1969)
Words and Music by Sonny Henry

Figure 1—Intro and Verse

"Evil Ways" came from Willie Bobo to Santana by way of their manager, Bill Graham. At the time, the Santana band indulged in long, unstructured psychedelic jams in which, as Carlos explains: "You couldn't tell heads from tails or bridge." Graham personally hand delivered and recommended the tune to Santana in his office at the Carousel Ballroom as if to say, "This song will get you airplay." Bill was right. "Evil Ways" became a hit that was played on both AM Top-40 and FM underground radio.

Immediately apparent was the rich, cross-cultured mix of rock, blues, Latin, and jazz music. The Gm to C vamp (i–IV) is a fixture in the Latin genre and recurs throughout the Santana repertoire. Carlos gives it a rock edge by rendering it with some gutsy, semi-distorted dyads in the intro. A case of less is more, he gets a lot of mileage from these two forms.

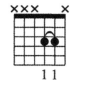

In the verse, Carlos applies a simple, but trademark, chord sequence in the Gm–C7–Gm–C7 changes. Notice that all three chords derive their common tones from one underlying minor shape, G minor in this case. The voice leading of D–E–F–E occurs on the second string. It's a move found in many Santana rhythm figures.

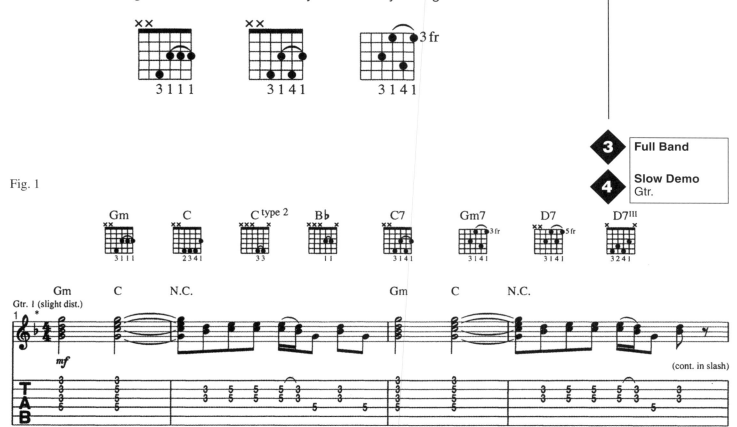

Fig. 1

3 Full Band

4 Slow Demo
Gtr.

* Key signature denotes G Dorian.

EVIL WAYS

Figure 2—Guitar Solo

The "Evil Ways" solo (3:01) is played over an animated version of the Gm–C vamp found in the verse and is filled with numerous signature elements. Santana splits his improvisational approach to incorporate both G Dorian mode (G–A–B♭–C–D–E–F) lines and G minor pentatonic (G–B♭–C–D–F) blues licks. He relies heavily on this shape which makes note choices from either scale source very accessible. The two notes of the Dorian mode not found in the pentatonic minor scale (E,A) are shown as hollow circles in the diagram while the black dots represent the notes common to both scales:

This is a very serviceable form which allows the extensions, the E note (6th of Gm, 3rd of C) and the A (9th of Gm, 6th of C), to be mixed freely within the lines.

Santana colors his lines with blues-inflected phrasing, bends, and vibrato. There are trademark ostinatos in measures 14–16, 16 and 17, 20 and 21, as well as the closing measures which exploit unison bends as still another ostinato riff. Notice the familiar Santana devices of accelerating rhythm in measures 20 and 21, and the characteristic syncopated pattern of eighth–sixteenth–eighth–sixteenth in measures 11 and 17.

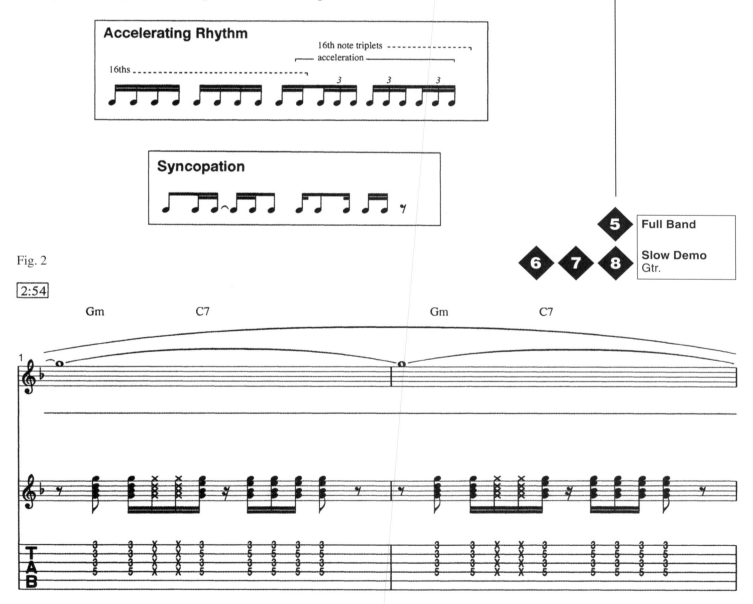

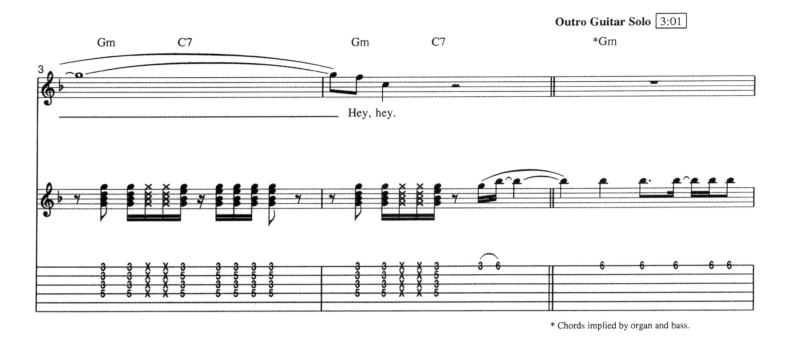

Hey, hey.

* Chords implied by organ and bass.

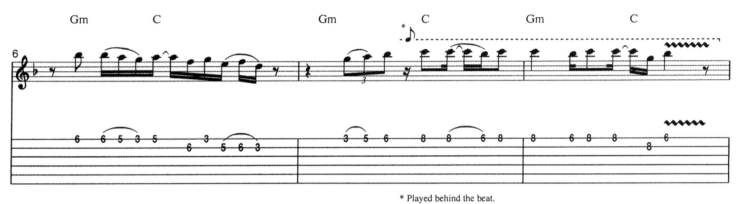

* Played behind the beat.

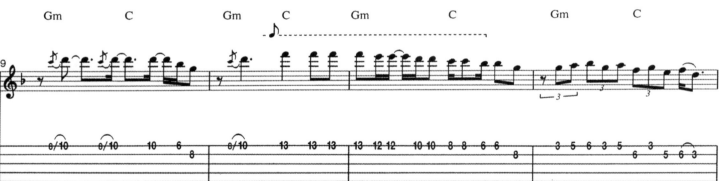

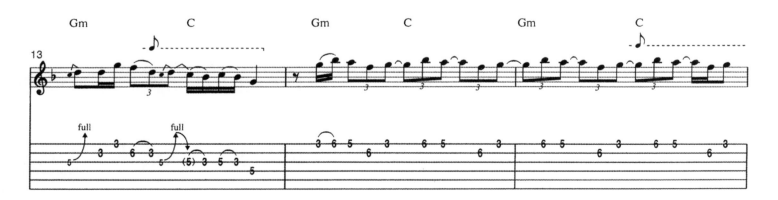

* Played ahead of the beat.

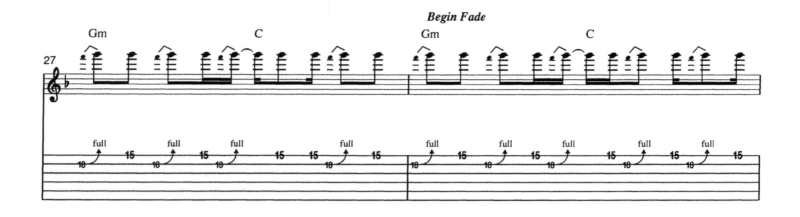

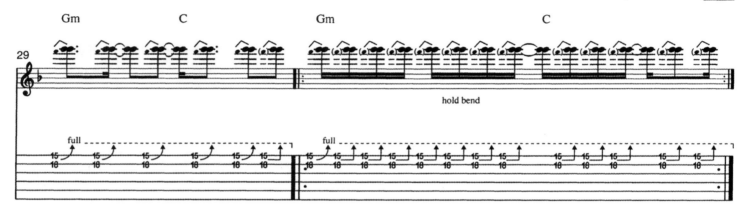

hold bend

JINGO (JIN-GO-LO-BA)

(*Santana*, 1969)
By Michael Olatunji

Figure 3—Intro

"Jingo's" uptempo Latin groove marries the rhythmic excitement of salsa to the power of hard rock. The vamp is derived from an underlying B Dorian mode, and is typical of Santana's use of the minor mode over a bass ostinato figure. Carlos's thematic melody in the intro solo (0:41) is played by two guitars of differing timbral characters—one semi-distorted, the other cranked to high distortion and sustain levels—serving as a perfect example of his application of simple guitar orchestration to the early Santana band tunes.

Santana's use of feedback sustain throughout this theme is unmistakable. Carlos describes his process for capturing and harnessing the overdrive of an amp this way: "I move back and forth until I find just the right kind of sustain. Sometimes I hear all these other overtones coming in, maybe out of tune [non-harmonic feedback]. I keep moving around until I get it. You find a spot between you and the amp where you feel that umbilical cord. When you hit a note, you immediately feel a laser between yourself and the speakers. It's like driving a real high-performance car. If you don't know what you're doing, you're going to be off the road. You have to practice with the intensity of the playing."

Santana follows this theme with a phrase that contains a signature trait (measures 9–12)—a statement which is more rhythmic than melodic (or at least equally so). Like a percussion pattern played as a B minor arpeggio on distorted guitar, it neatly capsulizes his Latin-jazz-rock synthesis into one tight passage.

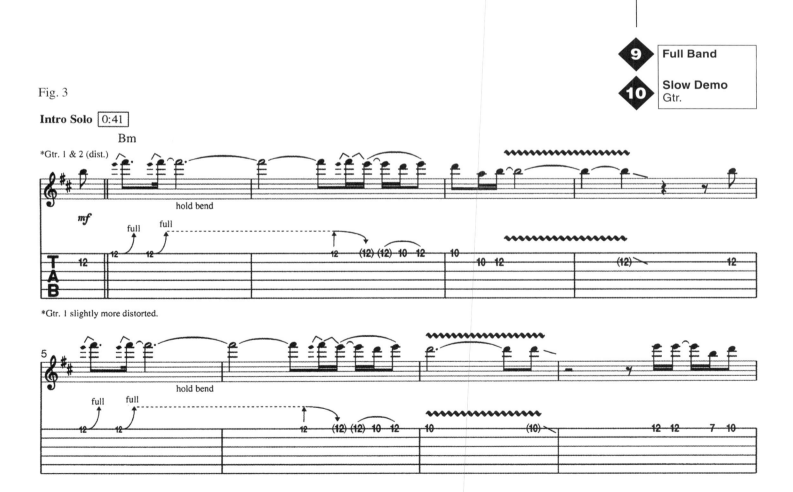

Fig. 3

Intro Solo [0:41]

*Gtr. 1 & 2 (dist.)

*Gtr. 1 slightly more distorted.

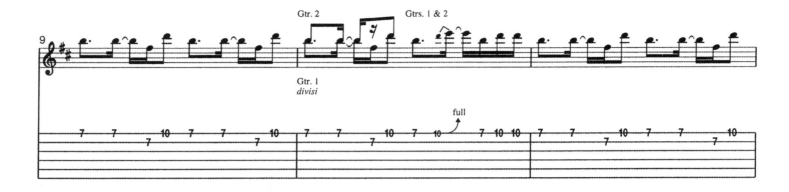

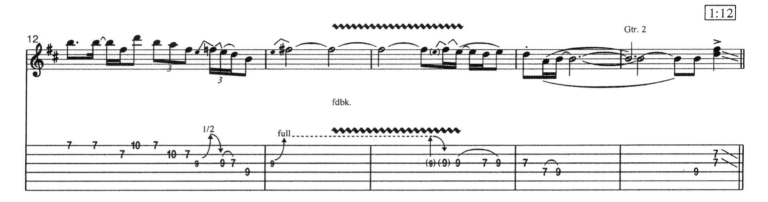

Figure 4—Guitar Solo

The internal solo section (2:45) opens by recalling the memorable theme of the intro, which is again played by two contrasting guitars. The ensuing improvisations, played by a single guitar, strike a healthy balance between blues licks and modal lines, blending Chicago blues and New York modal jazz influences in a Latin setting. Santana's improvisatory solo begins in the eighth measure, draws notes from B minor pentatonic and the B Dorian mode, and is firmly parked in the 7th position "blues box" form. Ostinatos abound, found in measures 9–11, 11, and 13. The latter is exemplified by rapid sixteenth-note sextuplet pull-offs which embellish the theme introduced in measures 9 and 10. Again, notice the jazz-influenced use of the ninth (C#), in addition to basic pentatonic melody, which produces a six-note, or hexatonic scale (in B minor: B–C#–D–E–F#–A). The blues licks in measures 14–16 create yet another ostinato—this time of unison bends played melodically. Santana concludes with an abbreviated recap of the theme in fragment form, further indicating the motivic thinking at work in his music.

11 Full Band

12 **13** Slow Demo Gtr.

Fig. 4

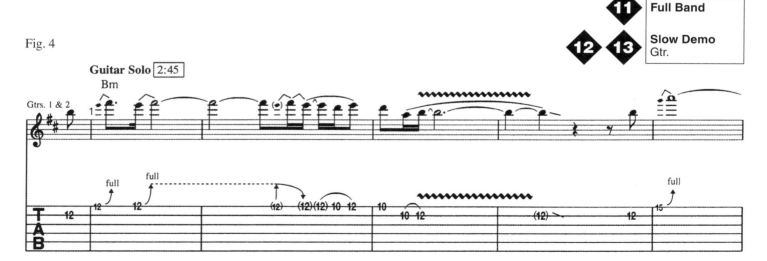

** Played ahead of beat.

* Played behind the beat.

SOUL SACRIFICE

(*Santana*, 1969)
By Carlos Santana

Figure 5—Intro

Santana was playing "world music" back in 1969—twenty years before it was seized as a fashionable buzz word in the nineties. "Soul Sacrifice" is incontestable proof. This immortal and definitive Santana instrumental overtly combines Latin and rock idioms. Santana-the man, the band, the music—simply *was* that—a natural fusion of intercontinental influences, as evidenced when the Woodstock festival audience of 400,000+ instinctively grasped and appreciated the fact. "The biggest door the band ever had the pleasure to walk through" could just as easily have slammed in their faces, but not with pieces like "Soul Sacrifice" in the set list.

In retrospect, "Soul Sacrifice" had it all; compelling percussion-driven Latin rhythms, powerful rock/blues/jazz grooves, joined-at-the-brainstem ensemble sections, and Carlos's soaring Pan-American guitar work. It begins with quiet (*mf*), sustained Am chords. The dynamics are increased to forte (*f*) for the main riff—typically solid and dyadic, based on a recurring A Dorian progression again delineating the i–IV (Am–D) chord sequence. Carlos's opening solo is legendary—comprised of tight, jabbing phrases that exploit space as a rhythm element, and set up a dialog impression, in measures 11–24. The phrases enter consistently on or near the "and of 3" in each measure, and utilize an imitative, question-and-answer approach. These call-and-response lines, made from A Dorian and A minor pentatonic melody, build by gradually ascending in register and gathering intensity to an inevitable and dramatic climax. Notice the sax-like legato line in measures 25 and 26, and characteristic syncopation in measures 27 and 28.

The four-measure figure (measures 29–32), composed of repeating A–F# and A–E motifs, is a perfect example of the Santana *signal riff*. Used to signal the point of arrival in a structural section, this type of "conducting" is an important organizational device present throughout much of Santana's output. The roots of this sort of procedure can be traced back to ancient African classical music (Sub-Saharan) and is an excellent technique for maintaining order within a group improvisation setting.

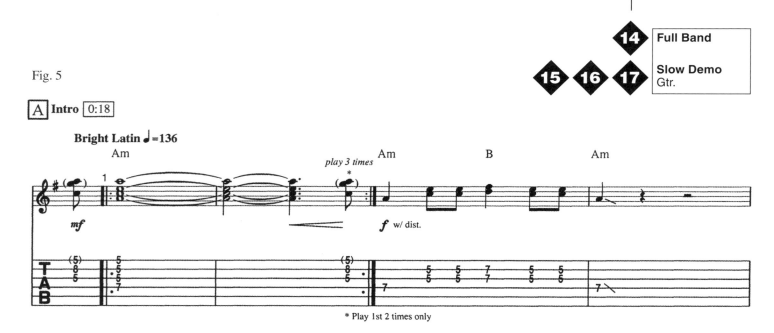

Fig. 5

* Play 1st 2 times only

** Chord symbols reflect overall tonality

* Played behind the beat.

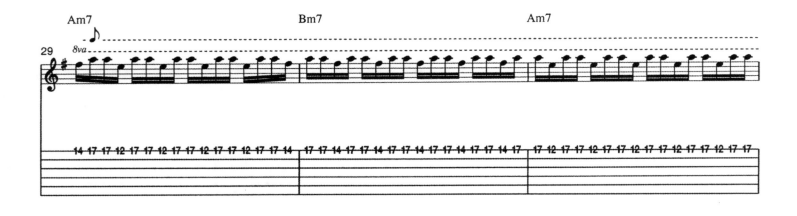

* Track 17 ends here

Figure 6—Interlude and Guitar Solo

The interlude is a melodious section with thematic lines that play off the initial organ part. The melodies move upward in an inversion-like manner—phrases imitating each other at different, chord-related pitch levels, forming a self-harmonizing effect.

There are a number of engrossing ideas in the solo (3:21), melding jazz, Latin, and Eastern sounds. Carlos begins with a syncopated ostinato riff in measures 13 and 14, which develop the closing signal melody of the intro. Check out the repeated-note, scalar descending line in measures 15 and 16, reminiscent of Santana's idol, Hungarian jazz guitarist, Gabor Szabo. The slurred modal riffs in measures 17 and 18, and the scalar ascending run (measures 19 and 20) evoke an Indian sitar-ish impression. The ostinato with open strings (measures 21 and 22) has an ethnic quality like near Eastern Bazouki music and again alludes to Gabor Szabo. Jazz guitarist Pat Martino, a later favorite of Carlos, is also fond of these types of sound and exploited them in his '70s recordings. Carlos closes with a signal riff based on a busier variation of the interlude theme.

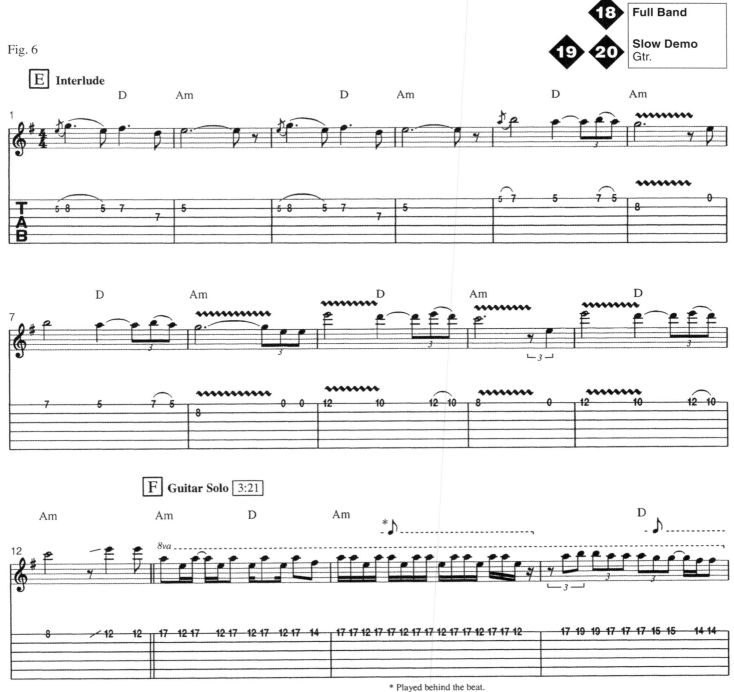

* Played behind the beat.

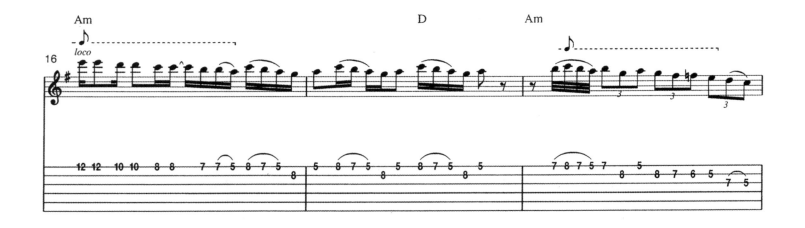

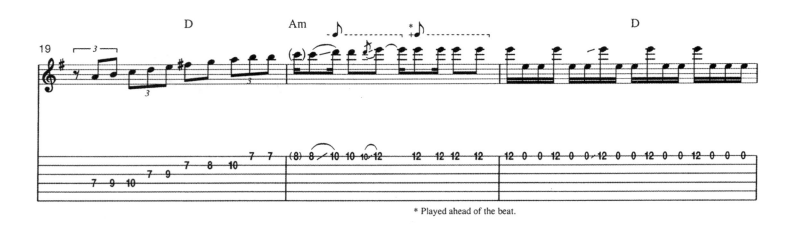

* Played ahead of the beat.

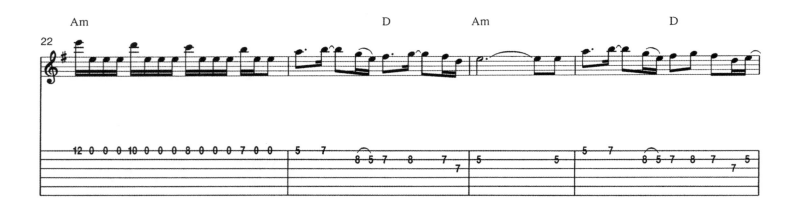

G **Organ Solo** 3:50

SOUL SACRIFICE

Figure 7—Outro

Carlos leads into the outro at 5:35 with a climbing A Dorian line articulated with slides and shifts. These rise steadily upward culminating in a tremolo picked high E, which functions as a signal to set up the outro ensemble section. The closing is largely rhythmic and is practically telepathic in the unity and tightness of the band's interaction. To say it builds is an understatement. It relentlessly rolls forward like the proverbial snowball effect—starting with a climactic eighth-note crescendo (measures 5–8). The main riff is recalled, and reinterpreted in measures 15–17 in syncopated form, playing off a familiar Latin dance figure. The final ensemble section (measures 19–24) exploits the accelerating rhythm idea as a band concept. Note the dramatic progression from halves and quarters to quarters with rests (same as staccato half notes) to pulse-based quarters:

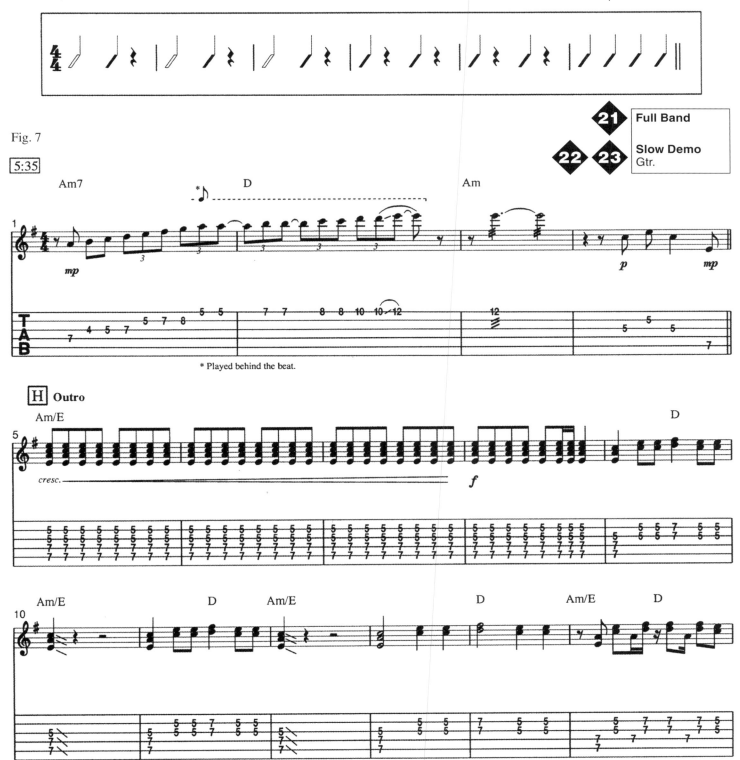

SOUL SACRIFICE

27

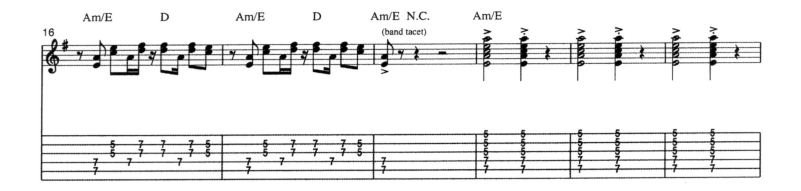

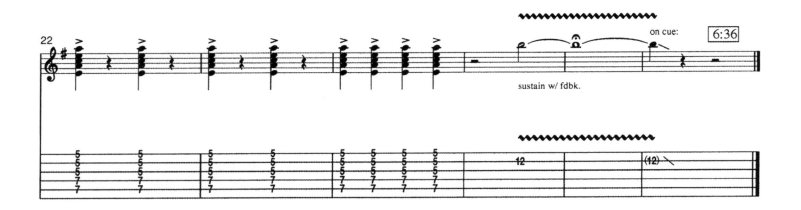

PERSUASION

(*Santana*, 1969)
Words and Music by Gregg Rolie

Figure 8—Outro Guitar Solo

"Persuasion" captures the harder rock side of the early Santana band. This Gregg Rolie composition also features some of Carlos's most exciting guitar work of the period. Case in point is the outro solo at 1:43. He begins his solo with controlled feedback and massive sustain as befits the song's aggressive blues-rock mood. The opening lines are played over a chunky and driving F minor riff (Rhy. Fig. 1) and contain some definitive Santana melody elements. Notice the deliberate use of the ninth (G) and the jazz-oriented slides in measures 5–7, in addition to the blues-oriented string bends and vibrato. The closing thoughts revert back to transplanted Chicago blues, complete with unison bends which signal the beginning of the climax. Here, short F minor pentatonic licks are inserted into the A♭m–Fm progression, arranged to function as if he were trading bars with the rhythm section—a well-known device in jazz improvisation. "Persuasion" ends thematically with a variant of the verse rhythm figure—a percussive riff made of aggressively strummed power chords and muted string scrapes that suggests a hybrid of hard rock, funk, and blues.

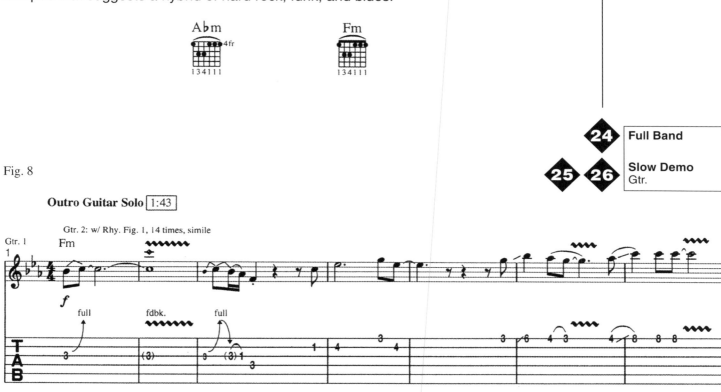

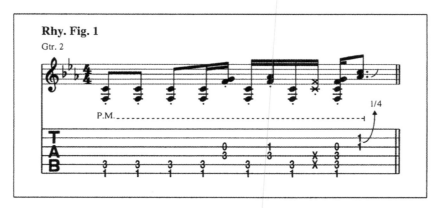

*Played behind the beat.

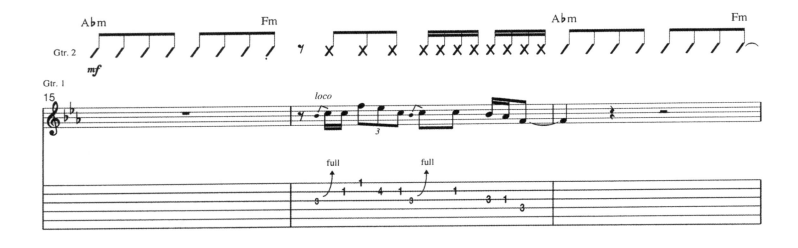

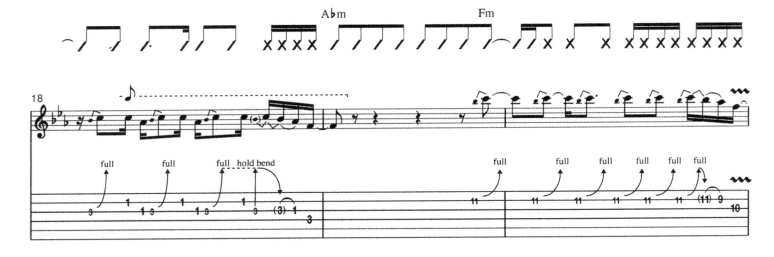

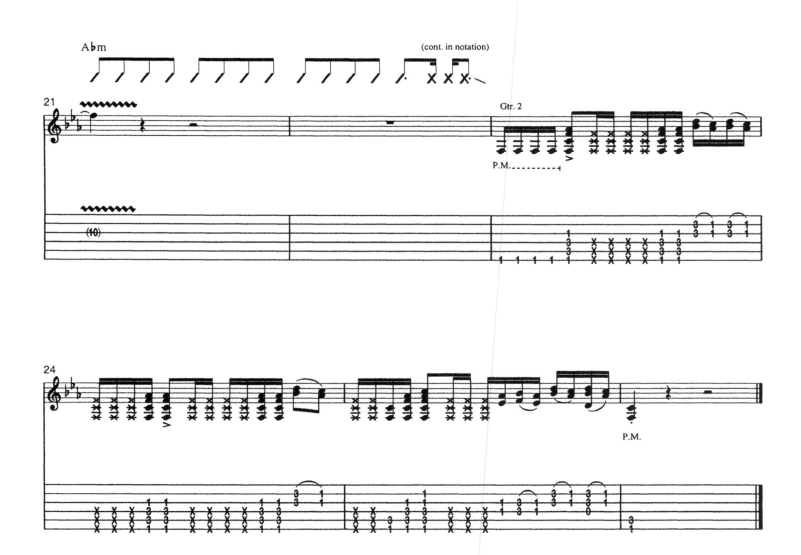

BLACK MAGIC WOMAN

(*Abraxas*, 1970)
Words and Music by Peter Green

Figure 9—Intro and Verse

"Black Magic Woman," from the landmark *Abraxas* album (1970), was a huge hit for the band. According to rock mythology, Gregg Rolie brought out the tune at a sound check in Fresno, California, and the band just immediately fell into it. The song, from the pen of British blues legend Peter Green (of John Mayall and Fleetwood Mac fame), has elements of classic minor blues like Otis Rush's "All Your Love," as well as Howlin' Wolf's "Who's Been Talkin'," but is strikingly original and attractive, especially as rendered by Santana. Introduced with an integral organ motif that grows out of the final notes of "Singing Winds, Crying Beasts," Santana's guitar work musically binds the texture and mood of the exploratory, spacey opening piece with "Black Magic Woman," as he builds from subtle slides and a restrained approach to a gutsy blues attitude. Note Carlos's trademark use of pentatonic and blues scale lines in a minor mode progression (Dm–Am–Dm–Gm); melodic inclusion of the 9th, E; and the overall warm, distorted tone.

The verse is filled with smooth Latin-inflected comping. Here, the chord changes are like an altered minor blues, with its reliance on the i, iv, and v (Dm, Gm, and Am) and its adherence to a 12-bar structure. Carlos's rhythm part is decorated with pull-off and hammer-on figures, muted strums, and variants of his familiar minor 7th-minor 6th chord pattern (on Dm: measure 6 and Gm: measure 8). This is found in countless Santana comping figures including "Evil Ways," "Soul Sacrifice," and many others.

Fig. 9

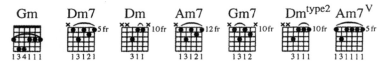

Intro

* Kybd. arr. for gtr.

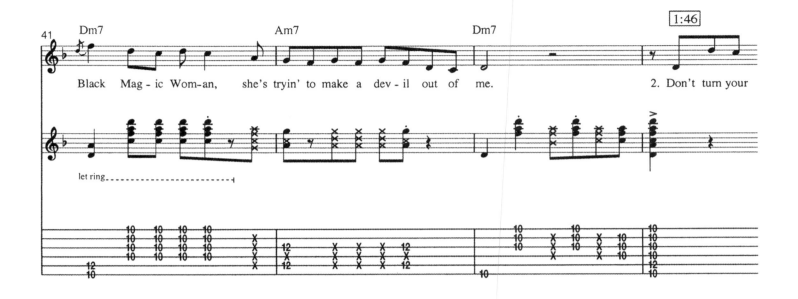

Black Mag - ic Wom - an,   she's tryin' to make a dev - il out of me.

2. Don't turn your

Figure 10—Guitar Solo

Carlos's internal guitar solo (2:08) occurs over two choruses of the song's changes. The melody of the intro solo is recalled thematically (in the second measure of each chorus) and reveals the motivic practices at work in Santana's improvisatory approach. This one involves a mix of blues and jazz ideas. The bends and phrasing are clearly blues-inspired while the consistent resolution to the color tone (ninth), E, is a jazz concession. Carlos exploits the D minor hexatonic scale (D–E–F–G–A–C) throughout his improvisations, which further emphasizes his jazz-oriented persuasions. The use of subliminal Latin influences can be heard in the break leading to the second chorus. Here, a phrase that contains a strong displacement of the beat, syncopation punctuated with very deliberate rests (typical in Latin music), is combined with Chicago-flavored blues string bends.

30 Full Band

31 **32** Slow Demo Gtr.

Fig. 10

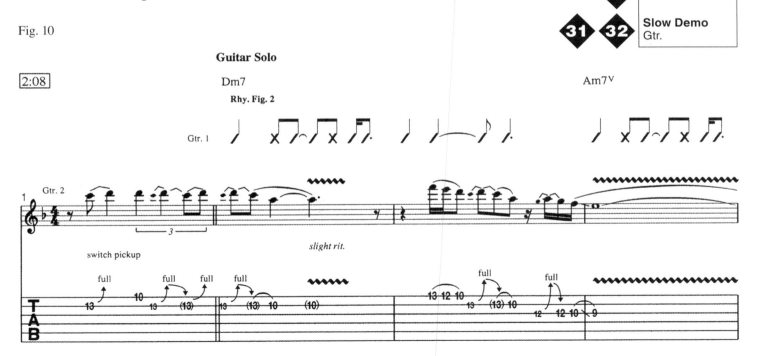

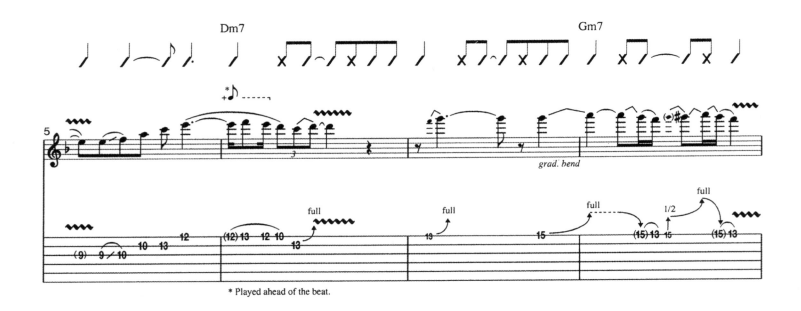

* Played ahead of the beat.

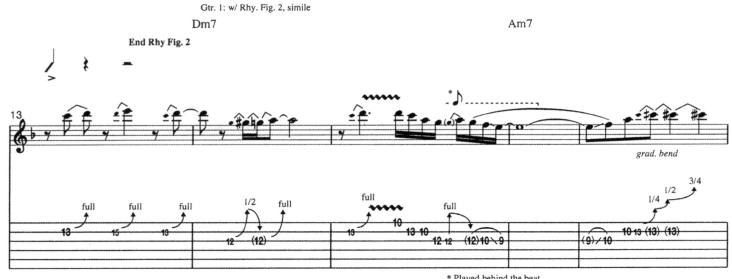

* Played behind the beat.

BLACK MAGIC WOMAN

Verse

Gtr. 1 w/ Rhy. Fig. 2, 1st meas. simile

3. You got your spell on me, ba - by, _____

GYPSY QUEEN

(*Abraxas*, 1970)
Words and Music by Gabor Szabo

Figure 11—Intro and Head

During the time of *Abraxas* (and somewhat earlier), Carlos was deeply under the spell of Gabor Szabo. It was only natural to reflect this obsession by moving directly, at 3:35, into Szabo's "Gypsy Queen" following "Black Magic Woman." A fragment of the intro (the organ motif) signals the segue into the opening measures of "Gypsy Queen," the second section of what will be a three-part cycle ("Black Magic Woman," "Gypsy Queen," and "Oye Como Va") combining the music of three genres and three influences—Peter Green, Gabor Szabo, and Tito Puente.

"Gypsy Queen" sits well in the Santana repertoire, and complements both the band's approach and Carlos's personal style. In it, one can sense the impact Gabor Szabo had on Santana. The piece contains elements near and dear to Carlos Santana—dramatic rhythm, ethnic modality, simple but effective tonal/chordal components, and solid riff-based ostinato phrases that are highly percussive in nature. The Szabo instrumental tune begins with a powerful, heralding theme, alternating between D–A–D–A, and sets up a change in mode to the parallel major, D major—in this case, the D Mixolydian mode (D–E–F♯–G–A–B–C), a major scale with a flat seventh (C). The head is stated over a droning D chord, which anchors the whole affair like the central tonic note of an Eastern raga, and proves to be an ideal setting for Carlos's terse rendering of the main melody and his feedback-laden guitar work. Notice the closing tremolo-picked high D which acts as a signal to cue the coda.

33 Full Band

34 35 Slow Demo Gtr.

Fig. 11

3:35

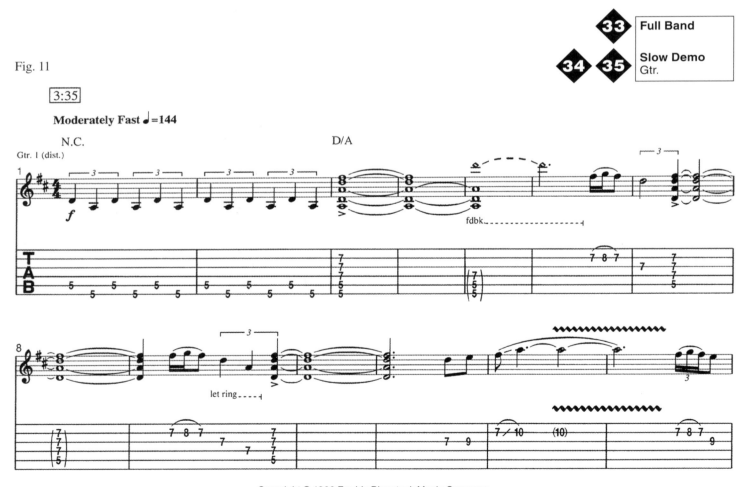

* Played before the beat.

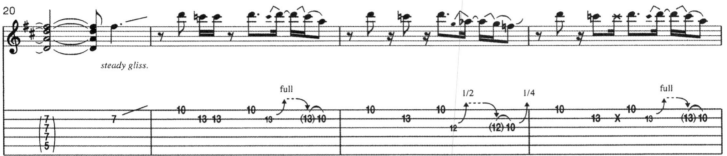

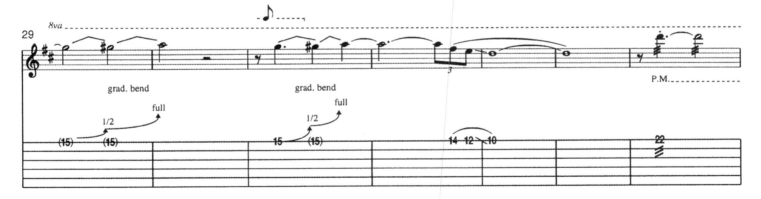

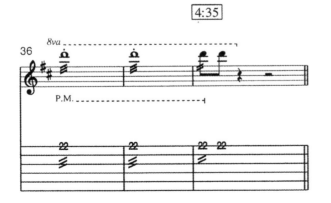

Figure 12—Ending

In the ending, or coda (4:37), chord changes are introduced which break the anchored modality of the head. These are C, G/B, and D, a progression which is found in countless rock songs, still clearly modal and derived from the D Mixolydian mode. Further rock elements can be heard in the heavy accenting of the changes, and an intricate, but driving, single-note riff that closes the piece.

Fig. 12

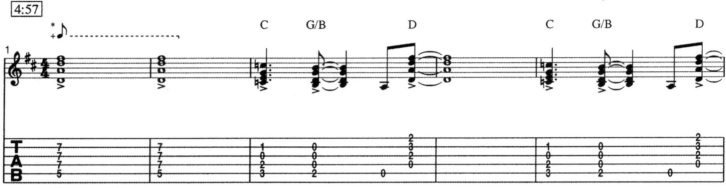

* Played ahead of the beat.

* Played ahead of the beat.

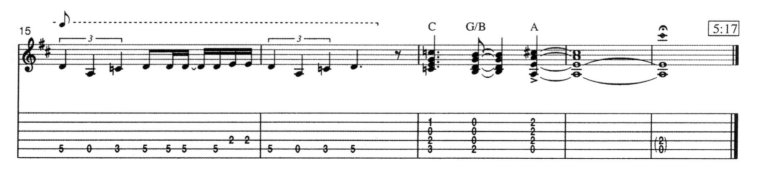

GYPSY QUEEN

OYE COMO VA

(*Abraxas*, 1970)
Words and Music by Tito Puente

Figure 13—Intro

Carlos Santana first heard "Oye Como Va" on the radio at around two in the morning back when he was living on Potrero Hill. It was a night of Afro-Cuban and Latin music (Ray Barretto, Eddie Palmieri, and Tito Puente). Upon first listen, Santana knew that there was something special in its insistent, percussion-driven groove and was determined to perform it. He wrote down the title, tracked down the record, and the rest is history. In Santana's "Oye Como Va," you get lost in "the dance of its groove." For Carlos, it is the epitome of hybrids—he often refers to it simply as, "It's church and it's also party." For others, it is the epitome of Santana—the type of Latin/rock crossover music that resonated so loudly with the public and created such a formidable audience for their unique style.

The mood shifts from the rock intent of "Gypsy Queen" to a more traditional Latin format in "Oye Como Va." This is ushered in by way of a signal riff, the hypnotic Am7–D9 vamp (another i–IV pattern), which is the foundation of the song and the backing groove for Carlos's opening guitar melody. Notice the jazz-oriented inclusion of the eleventh (A) and the ninth (B) as principal notes in this brief but memorable melody.

38 Full Band

39 Slow Demo
Gtr.

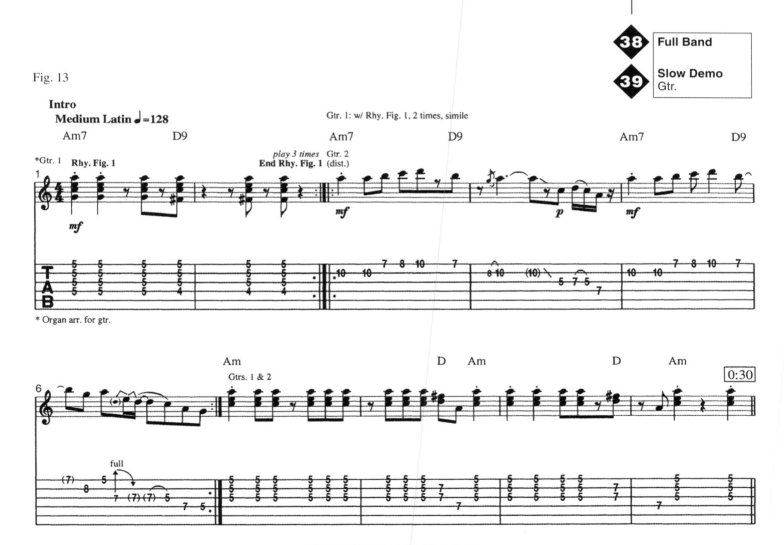

Fig. 13

* Organ arr. for gtr.

Figure 14—Guitar Solo I and Interlude

Santana's playing in the first solo (0:57) is filled with tasteful question-and-answer phrases and jazz-based references. He evokes impressions of Wes Montgomery, George Benson, and Pat Martino in the slurs from F–F♯ in the first sixteen measures. The melody is drawn exclusively from another hexatonic (six-note) scale in this section using the notes A–C–D–E–F♯–G. It can be perceived as A Dorian without a second (B) or A minor pentatonic with an added sixth (F♯). The latter view is also associated with modern guitarists Robben Ford and Larry Carlton. This melody reflects the underlying Am–D9 changes perfectly. At measure 17, Carlos exploits short, staccato figures of three notes or less for their intrinsic rhythm potential instead of longer melody statements. This produces the effect of the guitar functioning as a percussion instrument within the rhythmic fabric of the piece.

The following rhythm schematic illustrates this concept:

Notice the consistent shifting rhythm of the figure—it begins on beat 1, is next played on the and of 2, then on beat 4, on the and of 1, and so on. This is a strong technique for building energy and forward motion with an economy of melodic material.

The interlude (1:35) begins with a rhythmic melody comprised of sixteenths, eighths, and quarters outlining the Am–D9 changes. Note the percussive quality obtained by using a persistent repeated-note motif in measure 21. The rising chromatic figure (F♯–G–G♯–A) in measure 22 is also a solid rhythmic line. This is followed by an episode in measure 27 of arpeggiated chords in a stereotypical descending progression: Am–Am/G♯–C/G–D9/F♯. Played as a chord substitution against the implied Am–D9 framework, it is a staple of standard Latin and jazz music.

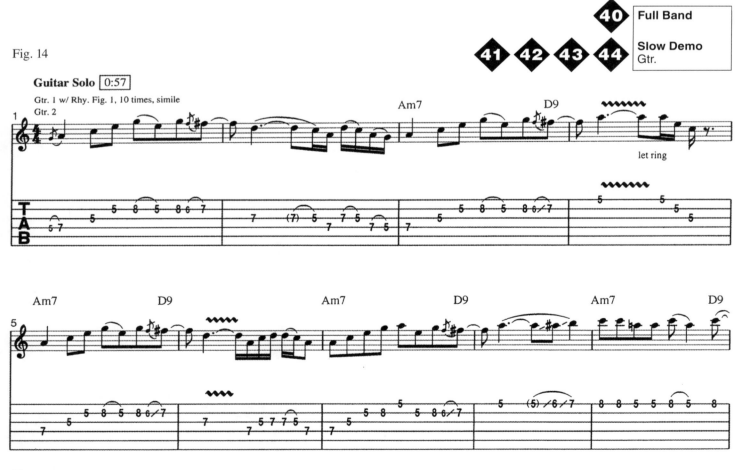

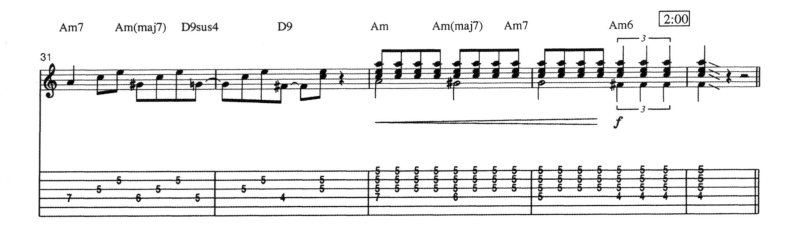

Figure 15—Bridge, Guitar Solo II, and Outro

Carlos recalls several elements from the first solo in his second solo (3:22). He begins by restating many of the ideas (i.e. question-and-answer lines) and phrasing, but soon adds some new wrinkles in the form of blues-flavored licks featuring bends and vibrato and aggressive double stops. The shifting rhythm motif from the first solo is recalled and functions again as a signal riff to conduct the final ensemble phrase.

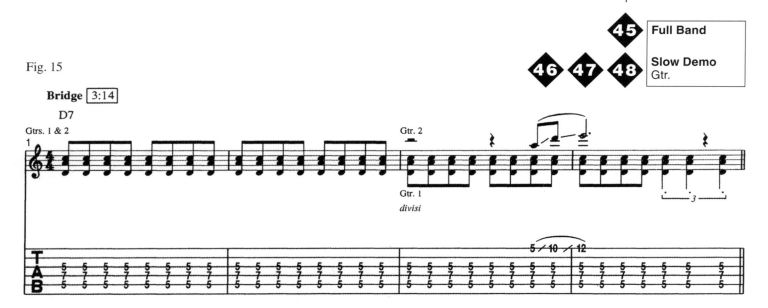

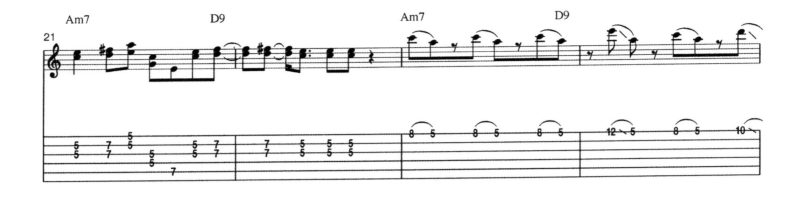

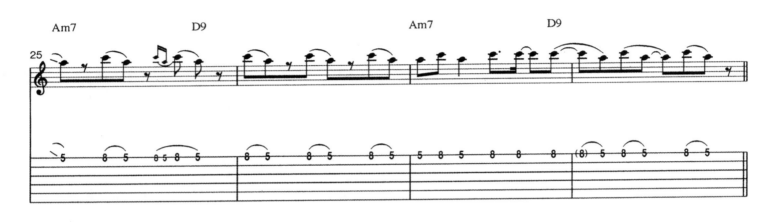

INCIDENT AT NESHABUR

(*Abraxas*, 1970)

Words and Music by Albert Gianquinto and Carlos Santana

Figure 16—Intro and Head

"Incident At Neshabur" plays homage to both the modal jazz school a la Herbie Hancock and Miles Davis, and the rock genre. The intro is based on a characteristic superimposition of triads (the contribution of guest pianist and co-writer Albert Gianquinto) over a G pedal figure in the bass line. This joins with a blues-rock figure in which the harmonic content of B♭ and C over G is retained and developed with a distorted hard rock tone on the guitar and a powerful, triplet-based ensemble part.

49 Full Band

50 Slow Demo Gtr.

Fig. 16

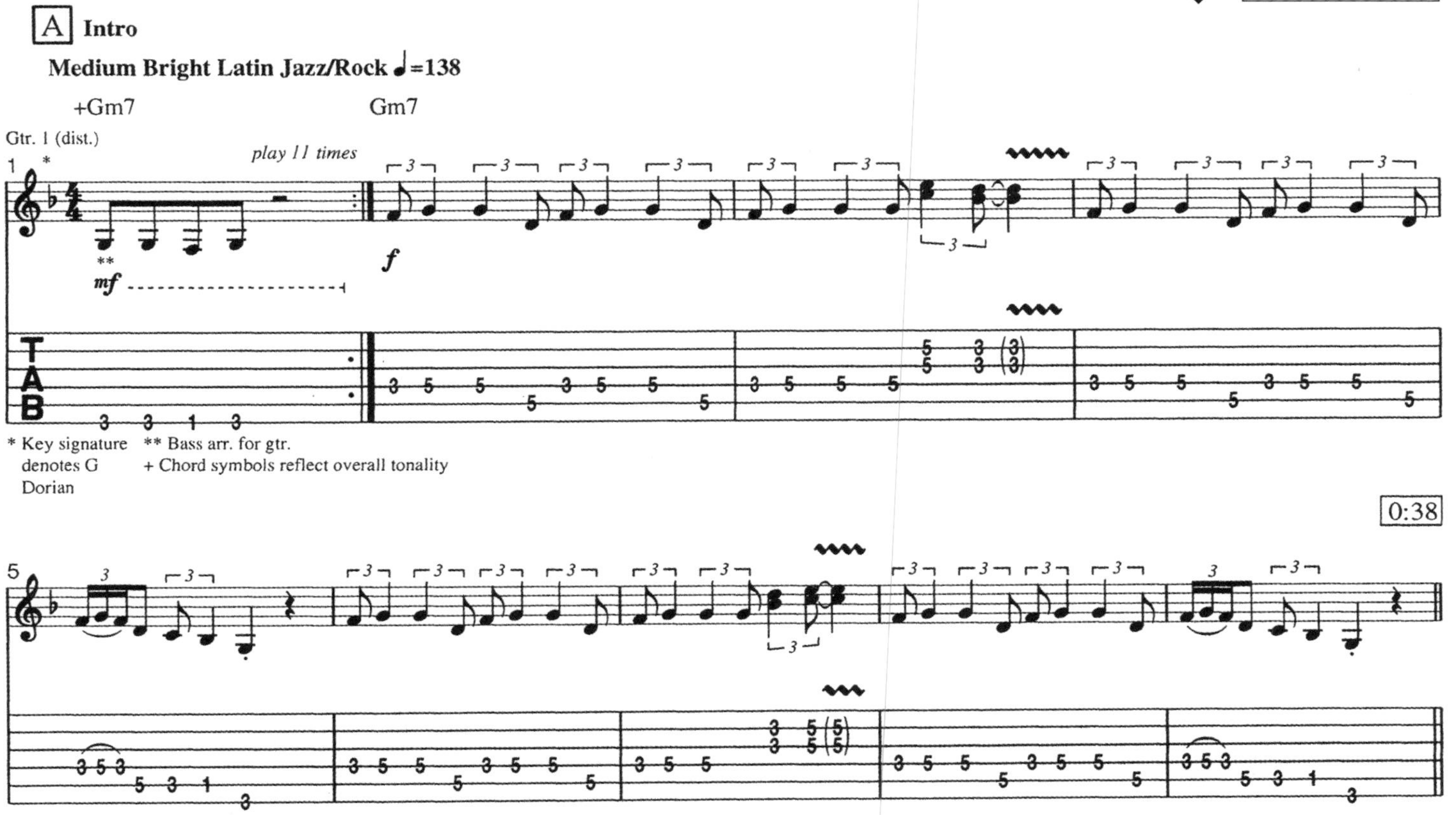

A Intro
Medium Bright Latin Jazz/Rock ♩=138
+Gm7
Gm7
Gtr. 1 (dist.)
play 11 times
mf
f
* Key signature denotes G Dorian
** Bass arr. for gtr.
+ Chord symbols reflect overall tonality
0:38

Figure 17—Guitar Solo

The opening phrase of the solo (1:51) reveals the jazz side of Santana's style. Notice the melodic emphasis on color tones (6ths, 9ths, and 11ths) as a way to impart an extended tonality on the first statement in measures 1–6, and the loping triplet rhythm of the lines. The solo continues in a jazz vein, exploiting motivic development through riff repetition, syncopation, and shifted rhythm. The final passage is noteworthy, utilizing blues-based sounds against the bebop-inspired cycle of fourths chord sequence of Gm7–C7♯9–Fm7–B♭7♯9–E♭9. Note that Carlos approaches these changes with two standard minor pentatonic licks: in D minor (10th pas.) over Gm and C7, and the other in F minor (1st pos.) over Fm, B♭7, and E♭9. It is a clever and resourceful solution for mixing rock and Chicago blues idioms within a decidedly jazz chordal setting.

Fig. 17

C **Guitar Solo** 1:51

*Key signature denotes D Dorian.

* Played ahead of the beat.
** Played behind the beat.

Slightly Slow

switch to bridge pickup

2:23

* Chord symbols derived from piano.

Figure 18—Interlude and Guitar Solo II

The interlude (2:28) flaunts a Dave Brubeck-style break which places a three-against-four figure into the arrangement, momentarily throwing a 6/8 feel into the proceedings. This was another of pianist Albert Gianquinto's contributions, and hints at the "cool jazz" movement of the fifties—providing a clever contrast to that which preceded.

The second solo is played against yet another rhythmic and harmonic background. Here, Carlos begins in a relaxed, quasi-balladic mood, in the new key center of C major. He improvises with great taste and restraint against a Cmaj7 to Fmaj7 progression. Check out the emphasis on dynamics as Carlos moves effortlessly from a pianissimo whisper to a wailing feedback cry in a single phrase. Open string pull offs a la Gabor Szabo (measure 11) are explored along with smooth legato lines, as well as funky, accented scale licks (measures 15 and 17) reminiscent of George Benson.

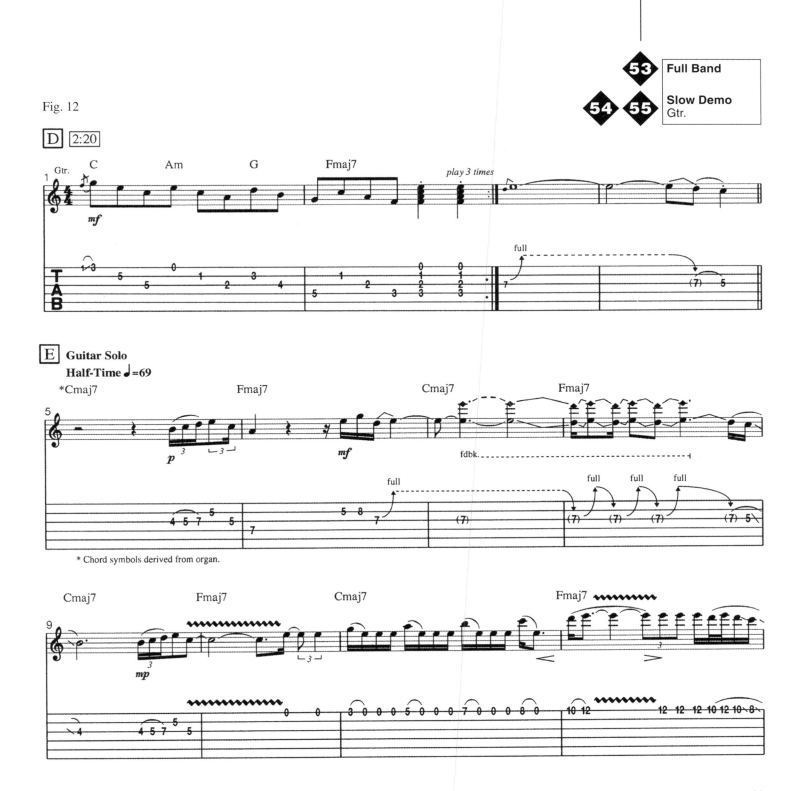

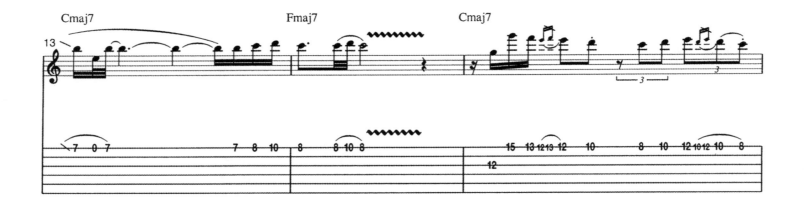

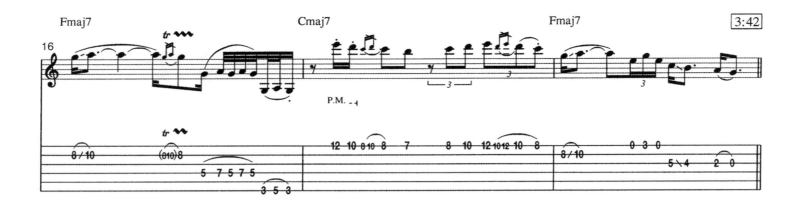

SE A CABO

(*Abraxas*, 1970)
Words and Music by Jose Areas

Figure 19—Guitar Solo

    "Se A Cabo" has the now-trademark Santana Latin jazz-rock fusion approach at its core. Carlos combines elements of blues and rock (bending and distortion) with jazz phrasing and note choices in his dynamic soloing over a driving Latin feel. We find numerous compelling fusion elements expressed in this solo. F minor pentatonic and blues sounds mixed with jazz concepts point to a clear case of B.B. King-meets-Trane over a Latin groove. Check out the sax-like legato run in measure 3 for example. The triad lick in measures 6 and 7 is another highlight. Here, Eb and Bb major arpeggios are superimposed over the F minor background for an extended-tonality effect; very much the sort of thing you'd expect to find in a modal jazz outing a la Miles Davis, John Coltrane, or Wes Montgomery. Along similar lines are the chromatically descending fourths in measure 8 followed by the B.B. King-inspired closing blues thoughts in measure 9—a truly eclectic moment in the eclectic Santana repertoire.

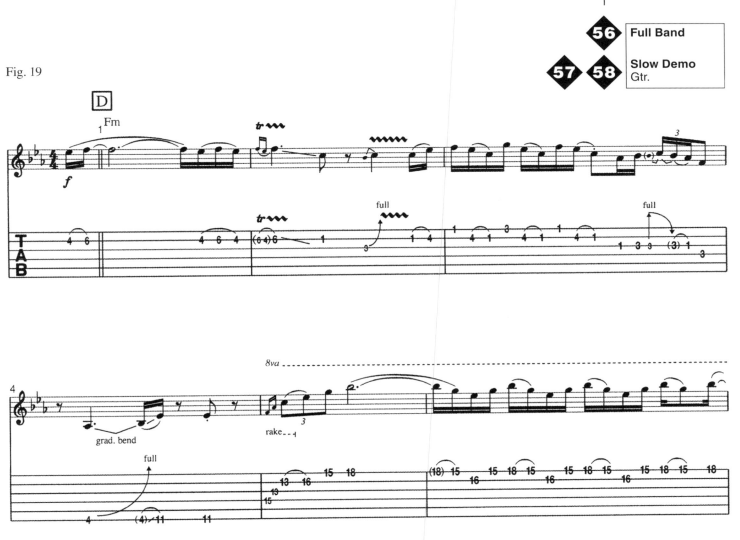

Fig. 19

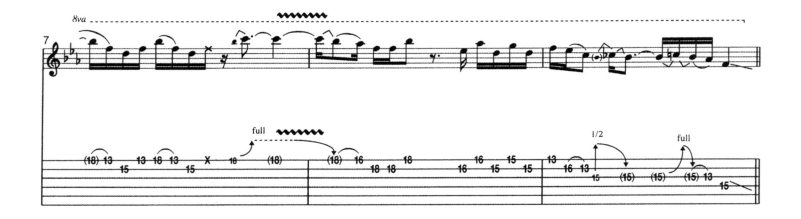

E

* Gtrs. 1 & 2

* Two gtrs. arr. for one.

F   1:30

SAMBA PA TI

(*Abraxas*, 1970)
Words and Music by Carlos Santana

Figure 20—Head

"Samba Pa Ti" is Carlos Santana at his soulful best. An instrumental masterpiece featuring his singing guitar voice, it is an unmistakable signature and a clear precursor of the classic "Europa," a later composition which similarly joins ballad jazz with Latin rhythm elements. Originally inspired by a few notes from a street sax player in the back alley near his room, it blossomed into a landmark Carlos Santana recording. "It was one of the first songs that I felt really free, free enough to forget about anything. You just let it flow through you. And even though it's very simple, there's still a lot of emotion in it." As if to reflect this personal view, the subtle nuances of his phrasing and embellishments of the theme defy description and transcend any categorization. Here, he is on par with Coltrane or B.B. King in terms of execution and emotion.

The song moves through cyclical changes, in either diatonic or cycle-of-fourths progressions—the harmonic basis for much jazz and Latin music, particularly the ii–V chord change. The head (verse section) consists of a G–Bm–Em–Am–D progression which Carlos interprets with a gorgeous and haunting rubato melody. Suffice it to say that he strikes a splendid balance between sophisticated jazz and earthy blues approaches. Check out the recurring outline of the Gmaj7 arpeggio (measures 1–2, and 5–6), use of the augmented fourth chromatic leading tone, slurs and ghost notes, as well as smooth, well-integrated hammer-on and pull-off articulation and tasteful, melodic string bends.

59 Full Band

60 Slow Demo
Gtr.

Fig. 20

* Chord symbols reflect overall tonality.

* Played behind the beat.

** Played ahead of the beat.

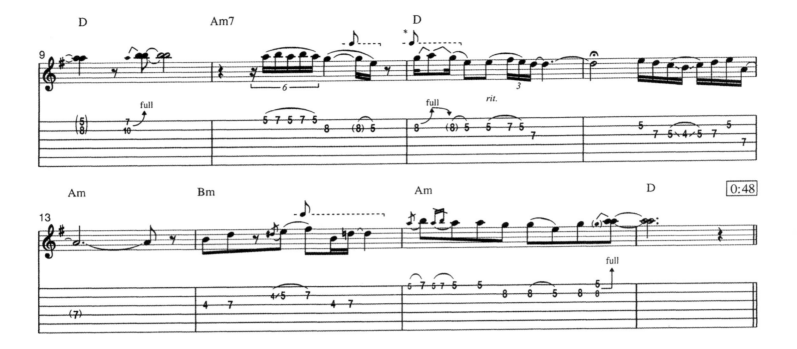

Figure 21—Bridge and Guitar Solo

The verse changes are contrasted and slightly elaborated in the bridge (1:39) with the chord progression of G–Bm–B♭m–Am–D, combining diatonic, chromatic, and cycle-of-fourths movement.

The ensuing guitar solo is a perfect example of Santana, the melodist. In his moving and exhilarating improvisations, Carlos brings together elements of light jazz, mellow rock, blues, and salsa to create a stirring musical offering. The improvising occurs over a G to Am chord vamp (Rhy. Fig. 1) in a double-time Latin feel. He skillfully mixes G major (G–A–B–C–D–E–F♯) lines with G major pentatonic (G–A–B–D–E) licks, and relative E minor pentatonic blues ideas, pursuing a compositional logic in solo construction with strong motifs and brief but memorable themes. Notice the pronounced use of syncopation, scalar lines with repeated notes a la Gabor Szabo (measures 32–33, and 41 and 42), slippery legato phrasing in his trademark one-string descending passages (measures 34 and 39), and aggressive pull-off flurries (measures 45 and 46).

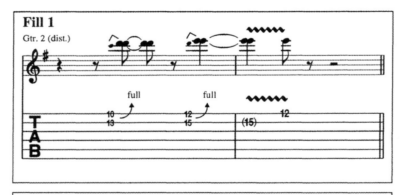

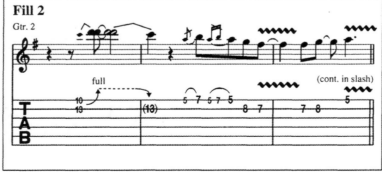

* Played behind the beat.

SAMBA PA TI

* Played ahead of the beat.

HOPE YOU'RE FEELING BETTER

(*Abraxas*, 1970)
Words and Music by Gregg Rolie

Figure 22—Bridge and Outro Guitar Solo

"Hope You're Feeling Better," another Santana piece penned by keyboardist Gregg Rolie, has a distinctly British rock feeling, and appropriately finds Carlos coloring his inimitable guitar lines with British blues rock and Hendrix influences. He builds up to the outro solo (in the bridge, at 3:04) with a definite strategy—beginning with a subdued, thematic E minor riff and the ensemble version of the main riff heard throughout the song. These two parts function as an eight-measure introduction to the freer and more florid improvising to follow (outro guitar solo). The groove changes, in the ninth bar, to a double-time hard rock feel which forms the perfect accompaniment for his energetic, blues-based passagework. Here, Santana employs E minor pentatonic melody almost exclusively, and decorates his Hendrix-inspired lines with searing string bends, vicious ostinato licks, and syncopated rhythms. The closing slurred chords recall a fragment of the inner solo (its last two measures), and indicates the thematic procedures present in the song's arrangement.

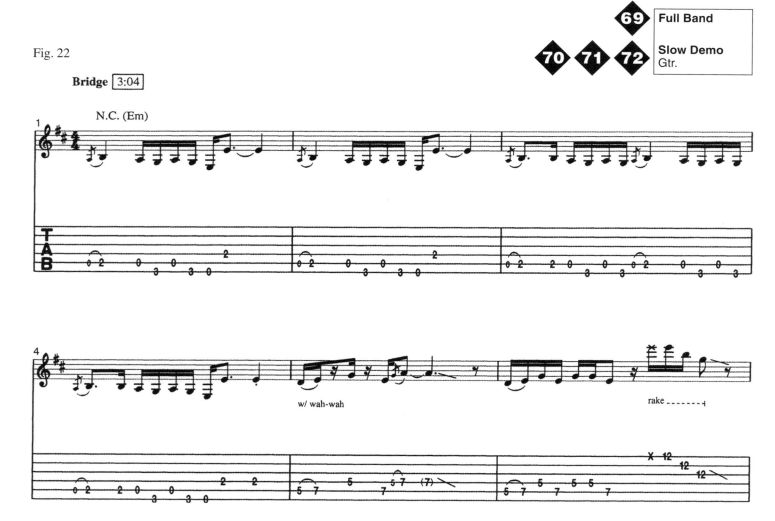

Fig. 22

69 Full Band

70 71 72 Slow Demo Gtr.

Outro Guitar Solo
Double-Time Feel

Em

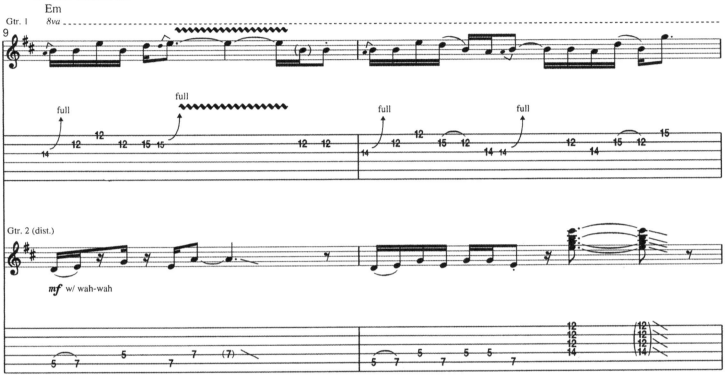

*Played ahead of the beat.

HOPE YOU'RE FEELING BETTER

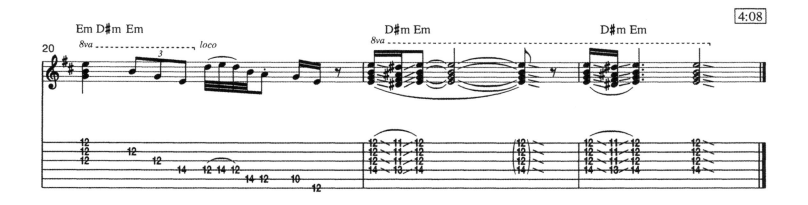

TOUSSAINT L'OVERTURE

(*Santana III*, 1971)

Words and Music by Michael Shrieve, Gregg Rolie, Michael Carabello, Carlos Santana, Jose Areas and Michael Brown

Figure 23—Intro and Head

"Toussaint L'Overture" was written to honor Toussaint, a military leader who successfully fought against Napoleon's troops in Haiti. "Before Waterloo, it was the only time Napoleon got his butt kicked. We did this tune for him, Toussaint," recalls Carlos with affection. It's essentially the same sort of Spanish chord progression that distinguished "Hit The Road, Jack," "All Along The Watchtower," "California Dreaming," "Stairway To Heaven," or "Mr. Crowley." Santana further said, "There are a million songs around those three chords. But for some reason, the way we did it, it sounds really different, even to this day," and he's right. Perhaps it's in the unique melody of the head and its note-to-chord relationship, the overall chemistry of the band, the supportive Latin-rock rhythm groove, or a number of other similar subtleties which determine its X-factor, a synthesis of it all.

The theme is half structured, composed melody, and half spirited improvisation over the Cm–Bb–Ab–G progression. A host of notable Santana elements abound. Check out the taut phrasing in the first four measures, a long sustaining, vibratoed cry in measures 5–7, jazz-oriented chromaticism in measure 9 flowing into a perfectly-phrased blues lick in measure 10, a rolling ostinato riff in measures 13–15, and predominate use of the ninth (D) as a significant melody note.

Fig. 23

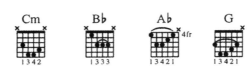

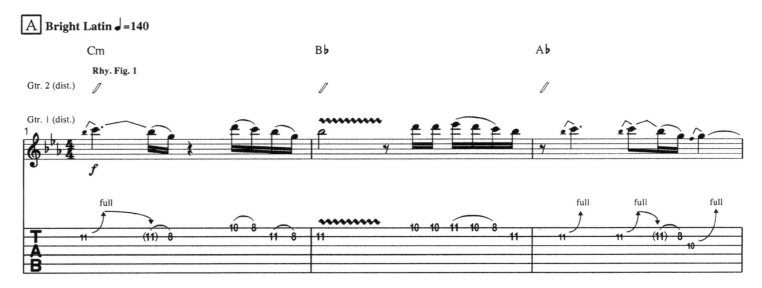

Figure 24—Guitar Solo and Interlude

A brief but exciting four-measure solo, begun at 1:47, introduces an interlude, or second theme area. This interlude is built from a series of consecutive riff sections in C minor. The first is stated by two guitars (Santana and Neal Schon) in dyads, with terse punctuations by Carlos in the holes between phrases, which produce an overall C minor mode soundthough not strictly adhered to. Note the prevalent use of the D+F♯ dyad which strongly suggests a Bm chord in C minor—not a standard minor mode relationship at all, but highly effective. The G♭ notes throughout in measures 5, 7, and 9 allude to the flat five of the C blues scale (C–E♭–F–G♭–G–B♭), an adopted orphan in the minor mode family, particularly in the rock, blues, and jazz idioms.

The second riff is an anchoring bass-line type rhumba figure while the third is a grooving middle-register ostinato (2:20) which splits the difference between accompaniment and song book. Note the presence of the the ninth (D) in all three sections, a Santana signature, as well as the characteristic Latin syncopations.

Fig. 24

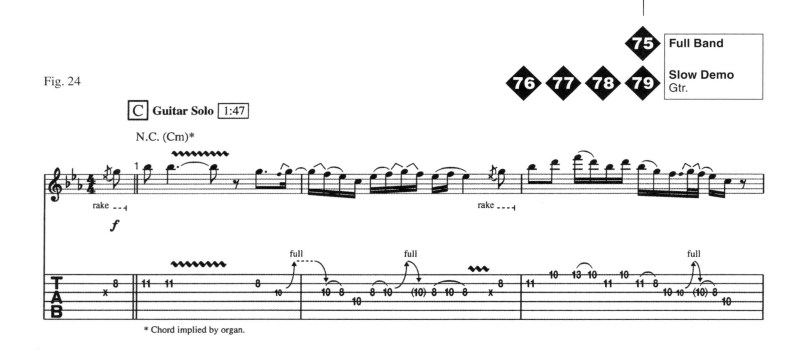

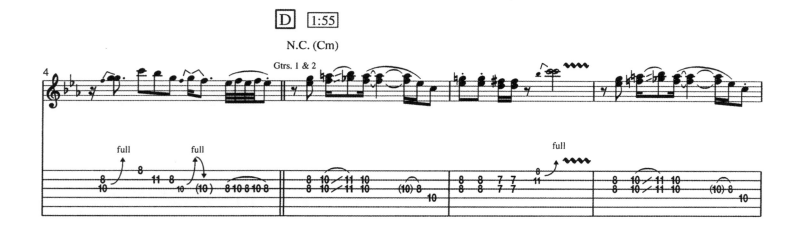

SONG OF THE WIND

(*Caravanserai*, 1972)

By Gregg Rolie, Neal Schon and Carlos Santana

Figure 25—Intro and Guitar Solo

When Carlos first heard "Song of the Wind" after it was recorded, he cried uncontrollably. Part of it was a reaction to the playing; he felt that both Gregg Rolie and Neal Schon played beautifully on the track. Another part was that it evoked a flood of memories—memories of the trials and triumphs of the band, the journey from Bill Graham and headlining the Fillmore to the Woodstock festival and their international success. But the primary tearjerker was Carlos's realization that the band had indeed ended, and that it was time for everyone to move on. *Caravanserai* represented the closing of a circle, and to Santana it was every bit as significant a record as *Abraxas*. Subsequently, the Santana band did disperse like leaves in the wind. Gregg and Neal left to start Journey, a progressive rock band that would attain mega-star status in the late seventies and eighties, and Carlos pursued new directions including duets with John Mclaughlin, a variety of solo projects, and a deeper spiritual quest with his guru, Sri Chinmoy.

"Song of the Wind" is a long, free-form jam based on a simple twochord vamp—just Cmaj7 to Fmaj7. Just? Over this streamlined pattern, Santana creates a beautiful piece of fretboard invention. It is virtually a pure stream of improvisational consciousness as licks become melodies, melodies become stories, and the stories are woven into the musical fabric of this large and elaborate musical tapestry. We are treated to a microcosm of his influences—felt in his references to the sobbing blues licks of B.B. King and Otis Rush, the fiery rock sequences of the British rock school, the boppish extended lines of Wes Montgomery, the jabbing repeated-note passages of Gabor Szabo, the buoyant Brazilian rhythms of Bola Sete, the funky R&B phrasing of Bobby Womack, and the floating modality of John Coltrane—all reinterpreted and retold with a master storyteller's skill and gift for communication.

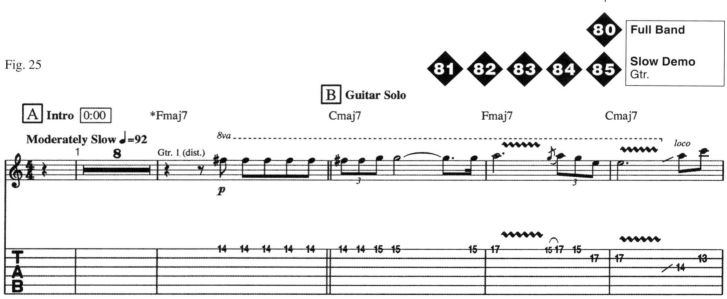

Fig. 25

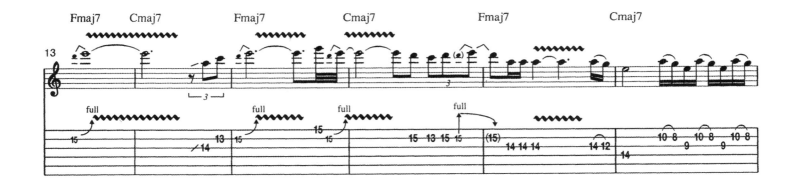

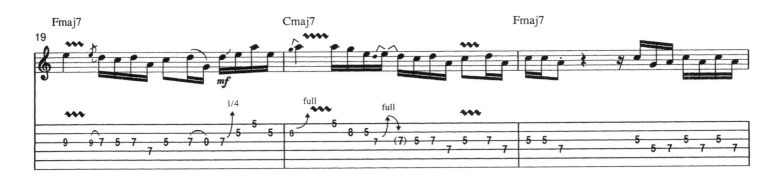

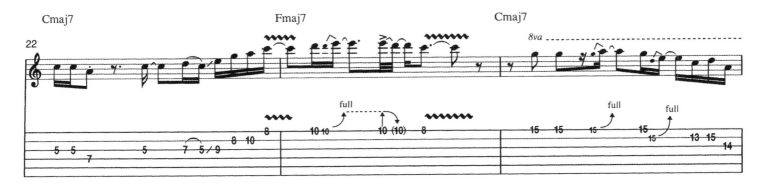

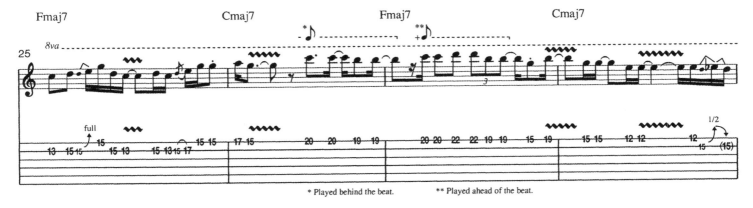

*Played behind the beat.   ** Played ahead of the beat.

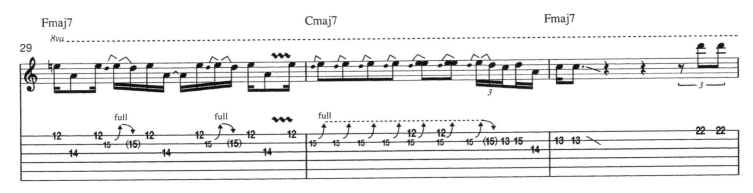

SONG OF THE WIND

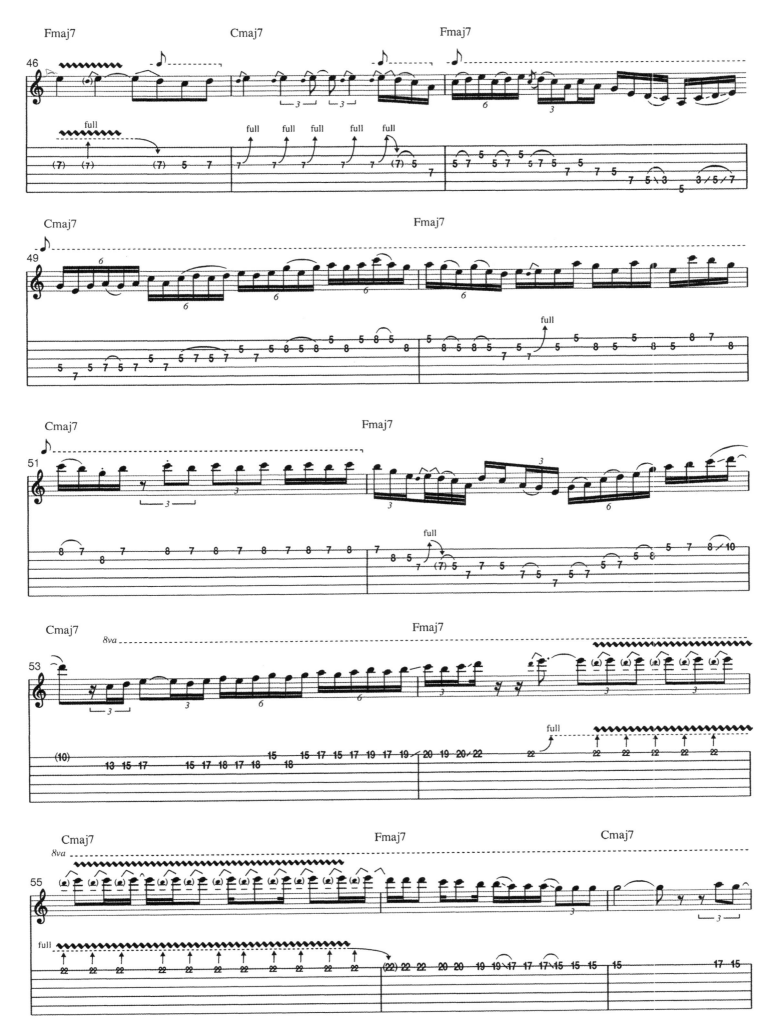

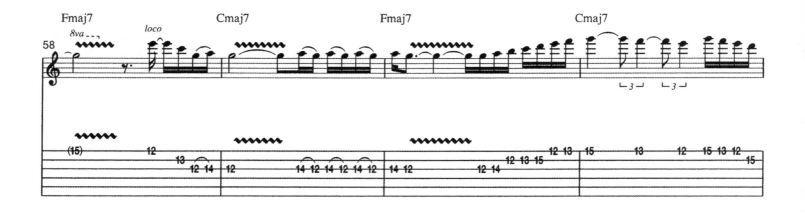

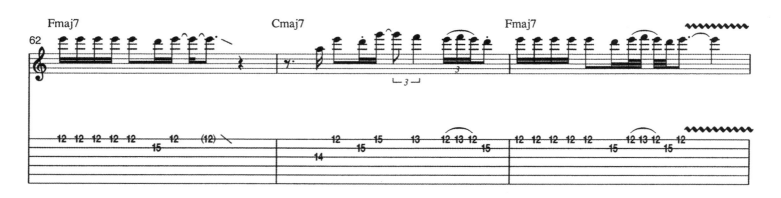

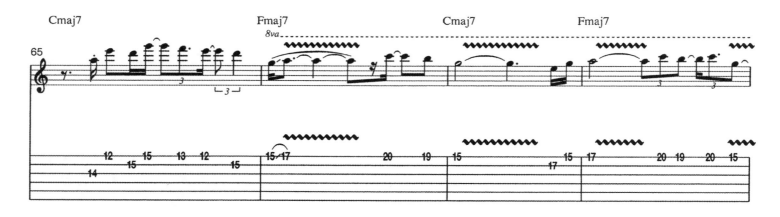

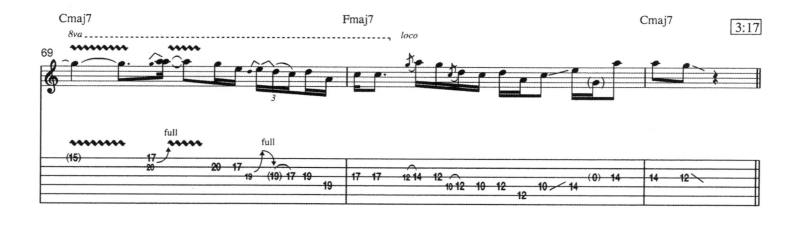

SMOOTH

(*Supernatural*, 1999)
Words by Rob Thomas
Music by Rob Thomas and Itaal Shur

Analysis by Chad Johnson

Figure 26—Intro

Released in 1999, *Supernatural* was the comeback album to end all comebacks. Although Santana had long ago attained legendary status as a guitarist with a singular voice, no one could have predicted the worldwide success of the album. The first in a series of albums featuring collaborations with numerous guest stars, *Supernatural* hit #1 on the charts on October 30, 1999, racked up eight GRAMMY Awards, and went on to sell over 15 million albums in the U.S. alone. Guest stars included Rob Thomas, Michelle Branch, Eric Clapton, Dave Matthews, Lauryn Hill, and several others. The album's lead-off single, "Smooth," was a Latin-sounding pop collaboration with Rob Thomas, who co-wrote the song with Itaal Shur. Featuring a cooking rhythm section and a dynamic horn arrangement, the song topped the *Billboard* Hot 100 chart for 12 weeks.

After a brief, stuttering drum fill, Santana joins in and kicks the song off with a pickup lick from the A minor pentatonic scale in 12th position. The two-measure chord progression of Am–F–E7 forms the bedrock of the song, and Santana mostly organizes his phrases neatly into two basic categories: long sustained tones over the Am–F measure, and scalar melodies over the E7 measure. Measures 2 and 6 are particularly telling of Santana's keen harmonic awareness, as he mines the A harmonic minor scale in 12th position and fifth position, respectively, to highlight tones from the dominant V chord (E7). As is customary for Santana, his tone is thick with sustain, and any note held for longer than a few seconds begins to give way to heavenly feedback.

86 ◆ **Full Band**

87 ◆ **Slow Demo** Gtr.

Fig. 26

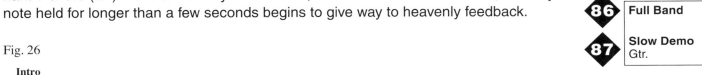

*Chord symbols reflect overall harmony.

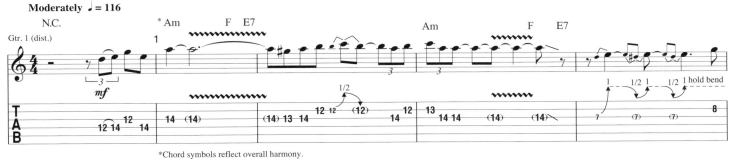

Figure 27—Guitar Solo

The guitar solo begins similarly to the intro, with the repetition of the two-measure progression of Am–F–E7. And much like the intro, Santana uses the familiar M.O. of sustaining chord tones over Am and crafting melodies from the A harmonic minor scale over the E7 chord. Note that, through measure 6, his lines can be distilled to two target notes: A at fret 14, string 3 for the Am chord, and G♯ at fret 13, string 3 for the E7 chord. In between these two are Santana's clever connecting phrases from A harmonic minor, which are variations of one another and can be seen as being derived from the E7 barre chord shape in 12th position.

At measure 9, Santana assumes the audience is warmed up enough and begins to cut loose by leaping into the higher octave. Still carefully targeting chord tones—mainly the root (A) over Am and the root (E) or ♭7th (D) over the E7—he makes his way up to the 17th-position A minor box by measure 11 and begins to phrase more freely. The pot begins to boil over in measure 12 as Santana climbs into the stratosphere and executes one of his patented picked trills between C and B in triplets, giving way to a tremolo-picked soaring bend from C to D in measure 14 over E7.

At measure 15, the progression changes to one that appears in the choruses (not shown), featuring a descending movement of Dm7–Dm7/C–Bm7♭5–G7–F♯7sus4–E+, all of which are diatonic to A minor, save for the last two. Santana capitalizes on the newly-injected momentum by riding a wave of soaring unison bends of G to A before locking in to a 16th-note descending run from A minor pentatonic in measure 16. As if to echo the chromatic horn ascent that occurs right before the solo (not shown), Santana bookends his own outing with a tremolo-picked chromatic line that spans from E to C♯ before resolving back to the tonic A on the downbeat of the following chorus (not shown). The first four notes of the ascent are played as octaves and demand careful fret-hand muting to allow for the tremolo-picking technique. Use your index finger for the notes on string 3 and your pinky for the notes on string 1. Allow the tip of your index finger to touch string 4, and deaden string 2 with the underside of the same finger. For additional insurance, you can lay your middle finger lightly across the top to quiet strings 5 and 6 as well.

88 Full Band

89 Slow Demo Gtr.

Fig. 27

2:49

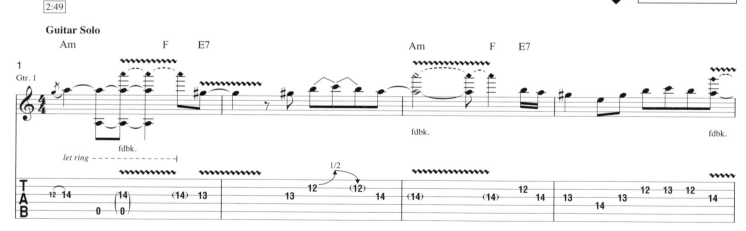

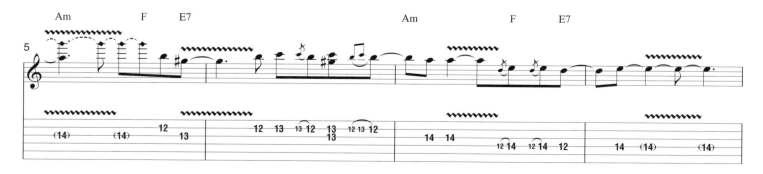

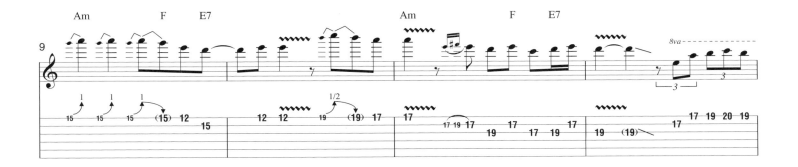

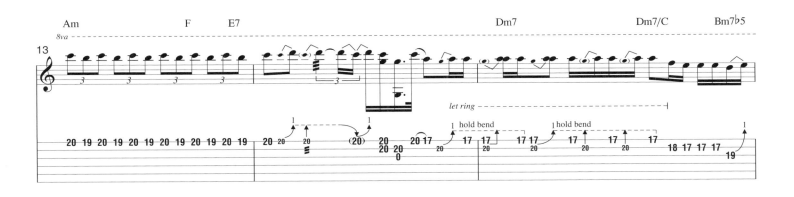

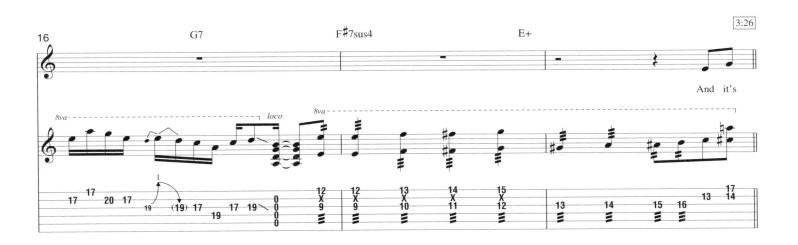

Figure 28—Outro Solo

After the chorus following the middle solo, Santana joins vocalist Rob Thomas with some ad-libbing over the Am–F7–E7 vamp, which continues this time until the fade. Working out of 12th position, Carlos again plays it very similarly to his previous outings at first, connecting sustained chord tones with A harmonic minor phrases over the E7 chord. Beginning at measure 9, we see evidence of his thoughtfulness as an improviser, as he works in a four-measure question-and-answer phrase. After pecking out the C/E dyad over Am in measure 9, he asks the melodic question by resolving to D (the ♭7th) over E7 in measure 10. After restating the C/E dyad motif in measure 11, he answers by resolving to E (the root) over E7 in measure 12. This seemingly simple device—a sign of musical maturity—is one that escapes many lesser players, content to simply echo one impressive lick after another.

Lest you think that he doesn't have any more tricks up his sleeve, though, Santana quickly dispels the notion. After a repeated three-note syncopated sequence of D–E–A in measure 14 gets condensed to simply E and A alternating in triplets, he lets loose with a high-register A minor hexatonic (A–B–C–D–E–G) assault on the top two strings. Freely mixing whole-step bends (from G to A on string 2 and C to D on string 1) and half-step bends (B to C on string 1) with tremolo picked notes, he ignites the heavens with his fiery phrasing and brings things to a fever pitch. With nowhere left to go, he begins to scale down through the A minor pentatonic box in 17th position, eventually finding himself back where he started again in 12th position, recapping his earlier moves from the beginning of the section.

After refueling with newfound inspiration, Santana begins ascending again in measure 25, this time up an A natural minor scale in 12th position. After reaching the end of that positional line, he leaps up into the stars once more with a dizzying series of sextuplet pull-offs on the first string—first with C–B–A in 17th position for nearly six beats. Just when you thought it couldn't get any more intense, he moves up to 19th position in measure 28 and peels off a few D–C–B sextuplet pull-offs before going for broke with a whole-step bend from D to E at fret 22, string 1, tremolo picking it into eternity for nearly two full measures. He rides out the fade from there, briefly dipping back down to the lower octave before returning to the upper realm as the track fades into the night. **Performance tip:** The sextuplet pull-offs in measures 26–28 are easy to phone in but harder to make sound *really* clean. Be sure that each note is distinct and clearly heard at a slower tempo before ratcheting up the speed.

90 Full Band

91 Slow Demo Gtr.

Fig. 28

3:43

Outro-Guitar Solo

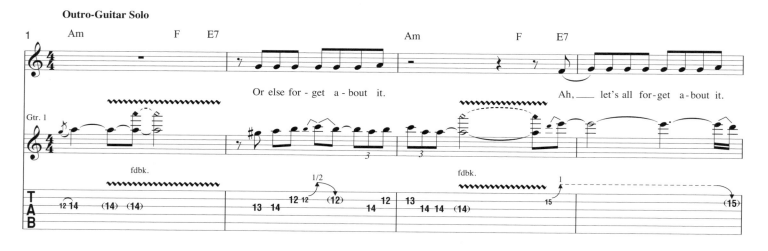

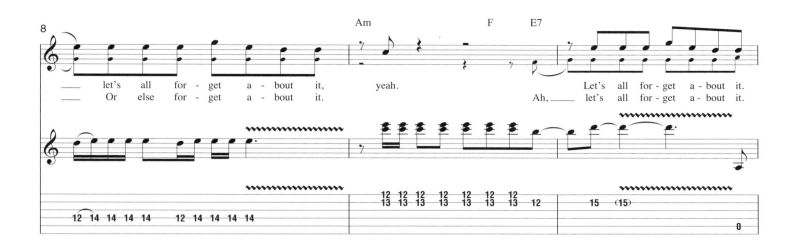

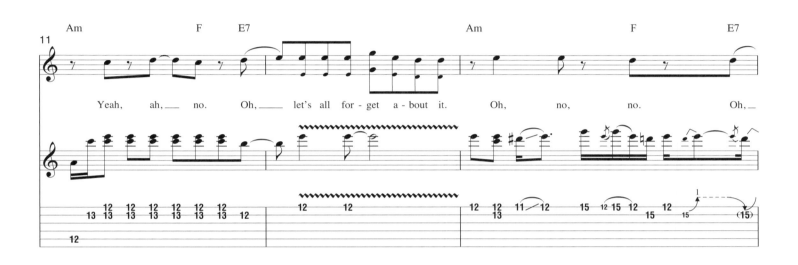

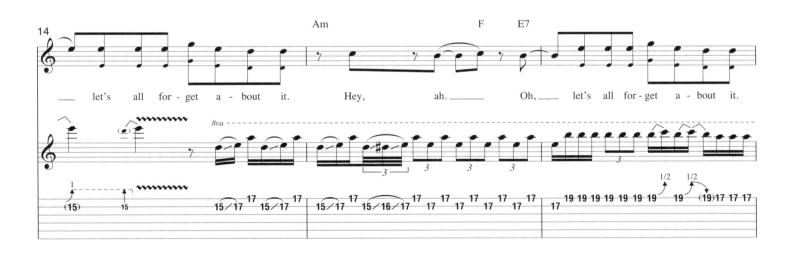

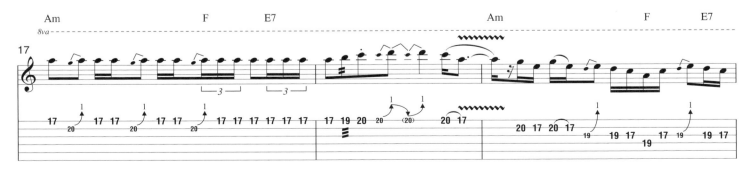

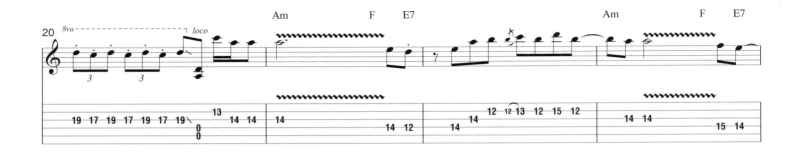

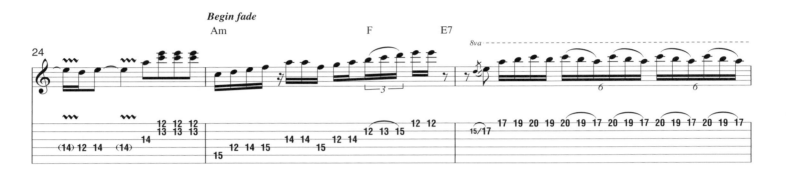

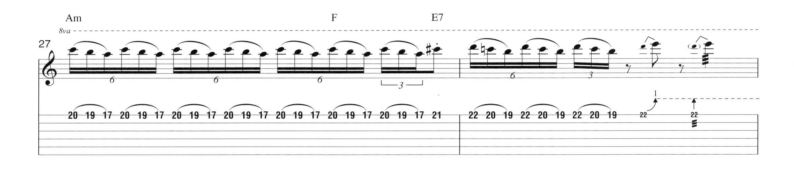

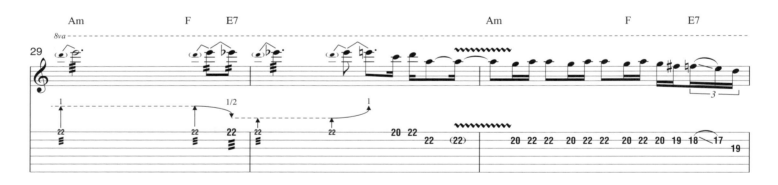

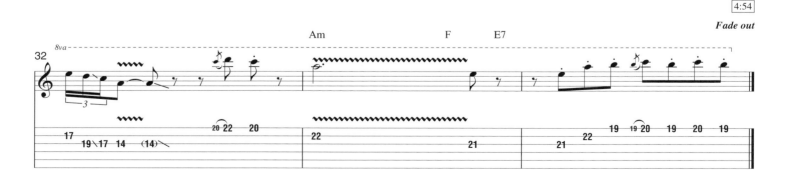

GUITAR NOTATION LEGEND

Guitar music can be notated three different ways: on a *musical staff*, in *tablature*, and in *rhythm slashes*.

RHYTHM SLASHES are written above the staff. Strum chords in the rhythm indicated. Use the chord diagrams found at the top of the first page of the transcription for the appropriate chord voicings. Round noteheads indicate single notes.

THE MUSICAL STAFF shows pitches and rhythms and is divided by bar lines into measures. Pitches are named after the first seven letters of the alphabet.

TABLATURE graphically represents the guitar fingerboard. Each horizontal line represents a string, and each number represents a fret.

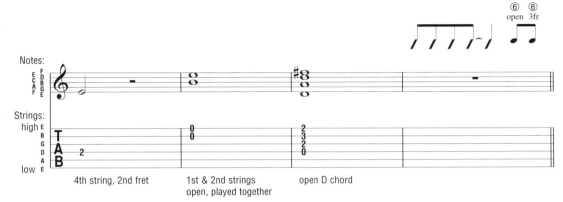

4th string, 2nd fret

1st & 2nd strings open, played together

open D chord

Definitions for Special Guitar Notation

HALF-STEP BEND: Strike the note and bend up 1/2 step.

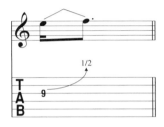

WHOLE-STEP BEND: Strike the note and bend up one step.

GRACE NOTE BEND: Strike the note and immediately bend up as indicated.

SLIGHT (MICROTONE) BEND: Strike the note and bend up 1/4 step.

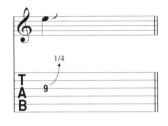

BEND AND RELEASE: Strike the note and bend up as indicated, then release back to the original note. Only the first note is struck.

PRE-BEND: Bend the note as indicated, then strike it.

PRE-BEND AND RELEASE: Bend the note as indicated. Strike it and release the bend back to the original note.

UNISON BEND: Strike the two notes simultaneously and bend the lower note up to the pitch of the higher.

VIBRATO: The string is vibrated by rapidly bending and releasing the note with the fretting hand.

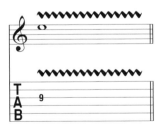

WIDE VIBRATO: The pitch is varied to a greater degree by vibrating with the fretting hand.

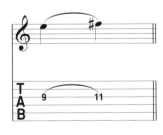

HAMMER-ON: Strike the first (lower) note with one finger, then sound the higher note (on the same string) with another finger by fretting it without picking.

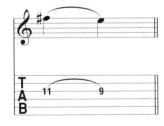

PULL-OFF: Place both fingers on the notes to be sounded. Strike the first note and without picking, pull the finger off to sound the second (lower) note.

LEGATO SLIDE: Strike the first note and then slide the same fret-hand finger up or down to the second note. The second note is not struck.

SHIFT SLIDE: Same as legato slide, except the second note is struck.

TRILL: Very rapidly alternate between the notes indicated by continuously hammering on and pulling off.

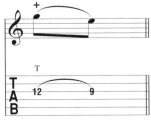

TAPPING: Hammer ("tap") the fret indicated with the pick-hand index or middle finger and pull off to the note fretted by the fret hand.

NATURAL HARMONIC: Strike the note while the fret-hand lightly touches the string directly over the fret indicated.

PINCH HARMONIC: The note is fretted normally and a harmonic is produced by adding the edge of the thumb or the tip of the index finger of the pick hand to the normal pick attack.

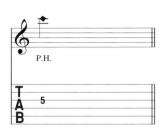

HARP HARMONIC: The note is fretted normally and a harmonic is produced by gently resting the pick hand's index finger directly above the indicated fret (in parentheses) while the pick hand's thumb or pick assists by plucking the appropriate string.

PICK SCRAPE: The edge of the pick is rubbed down (or up) the string, producing a scratchy sound.

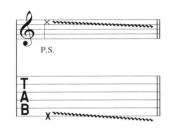

MUFFLED STRINGS: A percussive sound is produced by laying the fret hand across the string(s) without depressing, and striking them with the pick hand.

PALM MUTING: The note is partially muted by the pick hand lightly touching the string(s) just before the bridge.

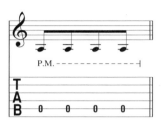

RAKE: Drag the pick across the strings indicated with a single motion.

TREMOLO PICKING: The note is picked as rapidly and continuously as possible.

ARPEGGIATE: Play the notes of the chord indicated by quickly rolling them from bottom to top.

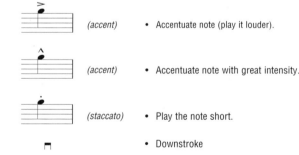

VIBRATO BAR DIVE AND RETURN: The pitch of the note or chord is dropped a specified number of steps (in rhythm), then returned to the original pitch.

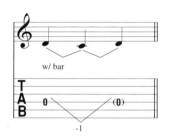

VIBRATO BAR SCOOP: Depress the bar just before striking the note, then quickly release the bar.

VIBRATO BAR DIP: Strike the note and then immediately drop a specified number of steps, then release back to the original pitch.

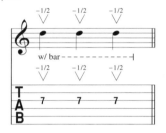

Additional Musical Definitions

> (accent)	• Accentuate note (play it louder).	
^ (accent)	• Accentuate note with great intensity.	
• (staccato)	• Play the note short.	
⊓	• Downstroke	
V	• Upstroke	

D.S. al Coda • Go back to the sign (𝄋), then play until the measure marked "*To Coda*," then skip to the section labelled "**Coda**."

D.C. al Fine • Go back to the beginning of the song and play until the measure marked "*Fine*" (end).

Rhy. Fig. • Label used to recall a recurring accompaniment pattern (usually chordal).

Riff • Label used to recall composed, melodic lines (usually single notes) which recur.

Fill • Label used to identify a brief melodic figure which is to be inserted into the arrangement.

Rhy. Fill • A chordal version of a Fill.

tacet • Instrument is silent (drops out).

• Repeat measures between signs.

• When a repeated section has different endings, play the first ending only the first time and the second ending only the second time.

NOTE: Tablature numbers in parentheses mean:
1. The note is being sustained over a system (note in standard notation is tied), or
2. The note is sustained, but a new articulation (such as a hammer-on, pull-off, slide or vibrato) begins, or
3. The note is a barely audible "ghost" note (note in standard notation is also in parentheses).